Just the Basics

Discovering the Truth in an Untruthful World

by

Danny G. Thomas

Commentary on The Revelation

of the Second Coming of Jesus Christ

To John the Beloved

FWB
Publications

For Worthwhile Books Publications

Columbus, Ohio

Introduction

For certain, the mystery of the return of Jesus Christ including the events of the last days is a subject that greatly concerns people everywhere, whether they are believers or not. What does the future hold?

The disciples of Jesus were continually asking about the setting of the Kingdom of God. In the **first** chapter of **Acts** verse **6** we read: *"Therefore, when they had come together, they asked Him, saying, 'Lord, will You at this time restore the kingdom to Israel?' "* **NKJV**. When Jesus ascended into heaven and the crowd there stood speechless, they were wondering about the question: "When will He return?" An angel addressed this question with those there that day by saying, *"And while they looked steadfastly toward heaven as He went up, behold, two men stood by them in white apparel, who also said, 'Men of Galilee, why do you stand gazing up into heaven? This same Jesus, who was taken up from you into heaven, will so come in like manner as you saw Him go into heaven."* **Acts 1:10 – 11 NKJV**

Paul dealt with the subject of the *Return of Christ* with the Corinthian church in **1 Corinthians 15** and the Thessalonian church in both books of **Thessalonians**. Peter and Jude addressed this subject as well.

Today there are too many ideas and opinions about the events that will happen at the *Return of Christ*, when they will take place, if they will take place, and the sequence in which the events of the "last times" will occur.

My purpose for writing this brief commentary is to merely look at what is written and not try to add to or to take away from what is written. In the last chapter, **Revelation 22:18 – 19,** John gives a warning: *"For I testify to everyone who hears the words of the prophecy of this book: If anyone adds to these things, God will add to him the plagues that are written in this book; and if anyone takes away from the words of the book of this prophecy, God shall take away his part from the Book of Life, from the holy city, and from the things which are written in this book."* **NKJV**

There are basically four ways in which the book of Revelation is interpreted:

1. **Preterist**: Most of the events happened during the first century of the early church.

2. **Historicist**: The events are an overview of church history.

3. **Idealist**: The events are symbolic and viewed as a conflict between Satan and God or good and evil in which God defeats Satan and overcomes evil.

4. **Futurist**: The events after chapters 4 – 6 are those that will take place at various times in the future.

I interpret Revelation basically from a Futurist point of view. The truth of the matter is, opinion is just that, "opinion." I know that what I understand about this subject will seem at times to be emphatic, but my desire is for the reader to just look at what is said and seek the Holy Spirit to gain a clear understanding from what is said. Someone has said: "It is not about what you feel, it is about The Truth."

In the flyleaf of one my Dad's preaching Bibles, he has written: "The task of the scholar is to guarantee the purity of the text; to get as close as possible to the Word as originally given. He may compare Scripture with Scripture until he discovers the true meaning of the text, but, right there his authority ends. He must never sit in judgment upon what is written. He must not bring the meaning of the Word before the bar of his reason." I do not know where this statement originated or who first made the statement, but I do know where I found it; and I do know for certain that my Dad lived by this guideline. I know firsthand that he preached in accordance with it.

Therefore, I wish to make my comments on what is written within the pages of the book of Revelation with this guide as my guide. Again, I have my understanding, but I do know for certain that Jesus is coming back bodily and at the exact timing that He has planned. I also do know that there are great concerns that all of us must have concerning the last times. I know that it will be a time where God pours out His wrath upon the world, Satan, and all those opposed to Christ.

I know that Jesus is coming for His children and His bride.

John 14:1 – 3: *"Let not your heart be troubled; you believe in God, believe also in Me. In my Father's house are many mansions; if it were not so, I would have told you. I go to prepare a place for you. And if I go and prepare a place for you, I will come again and receive you to Myself; that where I am, there you may be also. And where I go you know, and the way you know."* **NKJV**

I do know that God has not chosen the believer for wrath.

1 Thessalonians 5:9 – 11: *"For God did not appoint us to wrath, but to obtain salvation through our Lord Jesus Christ, who died for us, that whether we wake or sleep, we should live* *together with Him. Therefore comfort each other and edify one another, just as you also are doing."* **NKJV**

I do know that bad things are going to happen on this bad earth just because Satan, the prince and power of the air, is alive and well and is wreaking havoc upon the world and all believers.

2 Timothy 3:13: *"But evil men and impostors will grow worse and worse, deceiving and being deceived."* **NKJV**

I know that the fight of the believer is with Satan—principalities and powers on this earth—not people or flesh and blood.

Ephesians 6:12: *"For we do not wrestle against flesh and blood, but against principalities, against powers, against the rulers of the darkness of this age, against spiritual hosts of wickedness in the heavenly places."* **NKJV**

I also know the Jesus has overcome this world.

John 16:33 *"These things I have spoken to you, that in Me you may have peace. In the world you will have tribulation; but be of good cheer, I have overcome the world."* **NKJV**

So, with these things in mind, let's look at the "Unveiling" or the Revelation given to John the beloved by Jesus Christ.

Danny G. Thomas

Table of Contents

Chapter 1

Verses 1 - 3

In the setting of this book we find John, the son of Zebedee and brother of James (called Boanerges, the sons of thunder), **Mark 3:17,** the beloved disciple, **John 13:23,** who was exiled on the Island of Patmos.

The time of the writing of this book is around the time where John had been exiled to Patmos by the Emperor of Rome, Domitian, for preaching the Gospel around AD 95. John begins with the statement from which the title of the book is given: *"The revelation of Jesus Christ, which God gave Him to show His servants. . ."* **Revelation 1:1 NKJV.** The message was given to the servant of Jesus, or John, and delivered by Jesus Himself and another special angel from Jesus to John with a message for those who believe in Jesus and who are looking for His return. Those who are looking for His return are those who make up His church.

We also know the reason for the writing and that is the *"things which must shortly take place."* Perhaps it would be better understood as the **New Living Translation** renders it: *"events that will happen soon."* Shortly or soon, what does that mean? We read in **James 4:14:** *"whereas you do not know what will happen tomorrow. For what is your life? It is even a vapor that appears for a little time and then vanishes away."* **NKJV.**

Life on earth is fleeting. This life on earth is short and is temporary, but not so with God. We read in **2 Peter 3:8 NKJV:**

"But, beloved, do not forget this one thing, that with the Lord one day is as a thousand years, and a thousand years as one day." In other words, time means nothing to God because He is not bound by time in that He is "timeless." Time to God is like an eternal today or a forever present time. Time is not something that concerns God but "timing" is everything. We read phrases like, "in the fullness of time," or "at the allotted time," and then we also read: *"there should be time no longer,"* **Revelation 10:6 KJV.** One day, time will end, not by the actions of mankind but just as it began with the command of God in creation, **Genesis 1.**

With this understanding, it is obvious that Jesus is saying to John that God is about to give to him the sequence of events that will come at the last day. Believers of the first century church misunderstood Jesus as to His return because of their eagerness for His kingdom to be set up, and the church today still finds itself eager for His return and is wanting to know when He will return. We are to be eager and expectant, but we are also to be patient in our waiting for His return. It is with that mindset we patiently say, "Perhaps today." It could be at any moment. Jesus told us in **Matthew 24:44 NKJV:** *"Therefore you also be ready, for the Son of Man is coming at an hour you do not expect."*

John, who was the beloved disciple and was with Jesus while He was on this earth, who was one of the "inter-circle" of the three (Peter, James and John) who were always with Jesus, it was this John who is the witness of what Jesus and later the angel from heaven is about to reveal or uncover.

There is a special blessing that is given to those who read this message and that is to remember and take to heart what is written in this book for it will bless you. It will comfort you and increase your faith in time of persecution. This book is not meant to be confusing but comforting to the believer. Remember, John writes, it won't be long. Life is short, isn't it?

Verses 4 – 8

The recipients of the seven letters are the seven churches that were in the province of Asia which is the western border of the country of Turkey. The desire of John to these churches is grace and peace. To have peace, one must have a good sense of how he is perceived by others or by those who matter. John desires for the churches and the readers of this letter today to have a good understanding or perception of where they are and how they are carrying out the will of God in their lives. The grace that the believer has is given by God and His peace that passes all understanding is a product of that grace. God's peace and grace is a lasting peace and grace and can be believed and counted upon.

The letter is from Jesus Christ, the eternal and the Only Begotten Son, who is and was and is to come. It is from Him who is always faithful and is the Truth, the Way and the Life. Jesus Christ is also described as *"the firstborn from the dead."* In other words, He was the first to rise from the dead and secure for the believer an eternal life through that resurrection. It comes also from the *"seven Spirits who are before His throne."* The seven Spirits are mentioned only four times, **Revelation1:4; 3:1; 4:5 and 5:6** and more than likely each is referring to the Holy Spirit. Seven is the number of God, the number of perfection.

Jesus told His disciples that He was going to send the Holy Spirit to be their Comforter and Teacher and that the Holy Spirit proceeds or comes from the Father (**John 14:26**). God is *"the ruler over the kings of the earth."* He uses kings and their kingdoms to perform His will even in the midst of the Prince and Power of this earth, Satan. God draws lines in the sand which no one can cross. He is patient, gracious, merciful, loving, kind and, yet, He is just.

Not only does He use kings and kingdoms in His will and by His power, but He also loves us. He washes us and makes us clean in the sight of the Father. The believer is washed in the righteousness of Jesus in the blood that was shed for us as a final sacrifice. **Hebrews 10:14 NKJV:** *For by one offering He has perfected forever those who are being sanctified."*

The result of that sacrifice made us His children and able to reign with Him forever. What an awesome display of love that would take a sinful creation, dead in sin, and recreate it to perfection! **1 John 3:1**.

There is a reminder here that Jesus is going to return in clouds just as they saw Him leave. Though only a few people saw Him leave, *"every eye"* will see Him return. **Acts 1:11 NKJV:** *"This same Jesus, who was taken up from you into heaven, will so come in like manner as you saw Him go into heaven."*

Jesus left to prepare a place for us, **John 14: 1-3 NKJV:** *"Let not your heart be troubled; you believe in God, believe also in Me. In My Father's house are many mansions, if it were not so, I would have told you, I go to prepare a place for you. And if I go and prepare a place for you, I will come again and receive you to Myself; that where I am there you may be also."* And when He returns He will take us to be with Him and judge the unbelieving in His wrath.

As sure as God is, so shall it be when He returns. Jesus is, He always was, and He will always be. Jesus was before time began and He will still be when time ends. Jesus is God. Jesus is complete power lacking nothing. He is Almighty God.

Verses 9 – 22

The vision begins. The revealing of the last times begins to be described to John the beloved disciple who has been exiled to the Isle of Patmos and the rock quarries there by the Roman Emperor Domitian around A.D. 95.

John begins by reminding them of the common plight that they have with him. Every Christian will suffer. Every believer struggles and each believer will endure stress of various levels all through his sojourn here on earth. Struggle is not only something that a believer must endure; it is something that any living person on this evil earth must learn to deal with, to expect, and overcome. However, that struggle is much more pronounced for the believer for he represents Jesus Christ, and the principalities, powers, and workers of iniquity upon this earth are and will continue to intensify the struggle, playing havoc upon those servants of God.

We experience bad things, because we live on a bad earth, controlled by the "bad" hand of Satan but overcome by the "good" hand of God. The word "overcome" suggests that there is a struggle. Here in **verse 9**, John acknowledges his plight relating to the cause of Christ Jesus. He reminds the readers that he is:

- Their brother in Christ Jesus: There is no difference in him and them.
- Their companion in tribulation: There is no difference in him and them.
- Their companion in the Kingdom of God, heaven: The common destination of eternal citizenship.
- In a common struggle that requires Godly patience: Tribulation is required for patience to be developed.
- A common security: Victory is in Christ Jesus alone.

John's residence is on the small island of Patmos. It was not a residence of choice but by the hand of the Roman government for the crime of preaching the Gospel, the Good News that is found in Christ Jesus alone.

It was here on the Island of Patmos and on a Sunday that John was controlled by the Holy Spirit while worshipping and was given this "New Revelation." The voice he heard was the voice of Jesus Christ Himself. Jesus reminds John that He is the first, He is the last, and He is all that is contained in between. There is no time with God but there is "timing." God is all about timing but time means nothing to Him. We, on the other hand, only know time and experience the timing of God in life. We worry about time and complain about God's timing until it happens, and then we rejoice in that timing.

Here John is commanded to write down what he sees. John is not expected to "know about" what he sees or "understand" what he sees, but to merely "write down" what he sees and "send it" to the seven churches in the province of Asia, or what is known as Turkey today.

What John is about to see will confuse him, trouble him, and concern him greatly, but John's ministry here is to write and send only. That is something that every believer and minister of the Word of God needs to understand. We are called to "carry" the Gospel and proclaim the Gospel. How it is received, understood, and applied is the work of the Holy Spirit in the lives of the hearers and the personal choice that the hearers will make.

Success in the ministry is obedience only. Satan is the one who adds any other product. Some people may resist by spewing hatred, invoking physical pain, or spreading lies to cause discouragement. The obligation of the believer is to obey and be consistent and faithful in his obedience.

There are seven specific churches that are experiencing seven different problems. Each church is located in the province of Asia and each church will be receiving a personal letter. The churches are:

- Ephesus
- Smyrna
- Pergamos
- Thyatira

- Sardis
- Philadelphia
- Laodicea

The voice that John hears is unexpected and alarming. The voice identifies Himself as Jesus but is unmistakable as Jesus. He is standing in the middle of the seven lampstands or churches, and in His hands are the seven messengers, which I believe to be those called or selected to watch over the church as pastors perhaps. Out of the mouth of Jesus comes the Word of Christ which is like a "two-edged sword." **Hebrews 4:12 NKJV:** *"For the word of God is living and powerful and sharper than any two-edged sword, piercing even to the division of soul and spirit, and of joints and marrow, and is a discerner of the thoughts and intents of the heart."* **2 Timothy 3:16-17 NKJV:** *"All Scripture is given by inspiration of God, and is profitable for doctrine, for reproof, for correction, for instruction in righteousness that the man of God may be complete, thoroughly equipped for every good work."*

The sight causes John to fall to the ground but Jesus places His hand upon him and speaks peace. Jesus always speaks peace. Where Jesus is, there is peace, total peace; and so, we see Jesus speak peace once again to John.

Jesus is without beginning, without end, and He is before the beginning. Jesus is "The First," the first resurrection and alive forevermore. Jesus has the "keys of life and death." Jesus told his disciples that they were not to fear flesh and blood or Satan, but He who has the power to destroy eternally. **Matthew 10:28 NKJV:** *"And do not fear those who kill the body but cannot kill the soul. But rather fear Him who is able to destroy both soul and body in hell."*

Jesus has within His hand the power of (the keys of Hades and of Death) condemnation and commendation. Jesus has the power over Hell and Eternal Death. Did you know that every person that has lived on this earth or will ever live on this earth has an "eternal" destiny? All will spend eternity in God's heaven or in the place of torment that was prepared for Satan and his angels. Hell was not created for man but for Satan, but those who reject God's free gift of eternal life will be condemned to spend eternity with Satan and his angels. **Matthew 25:41NKJV:** *"Then He will say to those on the left hand, 'Depart from Me, you cursed, into the everlasting fire prepared for the devil and his angels.'"*

To live on this earth one "must be physically born;" there is no other way. God is a Spirit, **John 4:24 NKJV:** *"God is Spirit, and those who worship Him must worship in spirit and truth."* To live in God's spiritual and eternal heaven, one "must be born again" spiritually; there is no other way. The spirit is dead and must be made alive through the power of God and that power is unleashed through faith in Christ Jesus. **John 3:18 NKJV**. *"He who believes in Him is not condemned; but he who does not believe is condemned already, because he has not believed in the name of the only begotten Son of God."* **Acts 4:12 NKJV: "***Nor is there salvation in any other, for there is no other name under heaven given among men by which we must be saved."*

This is that name, that One who is speaking to John, and it is by His authority that this message is written.

The command to write will be:

> 1. The things that have already happened;

> 2. The things that now are happening;

> 3. The things that will happen in the future.

These future things are mysterious and difficult to understand. Yet, they are to be believed and expected. We do not have to understand, we must only believe and trust based upon the credibility and the truthfulness of the Word.

The sevens are:

The seven stars: Seven angels of each church and most likely the pastor of the church, in my opinion.

The seven golden lampstands: The seven churches.

Chapter 2

Verses 1 – 7

The church at Ephesus: The loveless church.

Jesus describes himself as: *"He who holds the seven stars in His right hand, who walks in the midst of the seven golden lampstands,"* **Verse 1, NKJV.** Jesus is in control and He also is fully aware of all things. He is in the battle with us, He holds us, and He attends to us.

Ephesus was the city where Paul spent more time than he had at any other church, about three years. **Acts 20:31:** *"Therefore watch, and remember that for three years I did not cease to warn everyone night and day with tears,"* **NKJV.** Ephesus was where Paul met a group of Gentile disciples who had not been baptized by the Holy Spirit. They knew nothing about the Holy Spirit, they admitted, and Paul then laid his hands upon them, and they received the Holy Spirit. **Acts 19:1-10.**

Paul wrote a detailed Epistle to this church to strengthen them, equip them, and encourage them to be steadfast and stand against the wiles of the devil; but in fewer than thirty years later, they "have left their first love," **Verse 4.**

John writes that Jesus knows of the accomplishments that they made: They were hard workers; they were tested by persecution and remained faithful and true to the Gospel; they were careful of those who might come into the church with a false doctrine or hidden agendas, and they faithfully exposed them for what they were. They were standing firm, but what has happened? They had become critical of other believers and the love that they once had for Jesus and others had weakened somehow.

What had happened is they had taken their eyes off Jesus and placed them upon the knowledge that they had. They were more confident in themselves and what they had done than in Jesus and what He had done for them and the love that He had placed within them. They had fallen a long way from where they once were. Jesus says: *"Remember therefore from where you have fallen;"* **Vs. 5.**

The needed remedy was to remember, admit, and acknowledge where they were, and then to return or repent to where they once were. Repentance is turning around. The challenge to us is to be careful of our criticism of others and to be concerned with our love for Jesus. Why do you serve Jesus? Are you serving for recognition? Are you offended when you are not recognized for deeds and accomplishments within your body of believers? It's not about you after all. It is about two things: (1) Him, and (2) Them. To fail to return will result in the death of the church.

There was one additional quality which was that they hated the doctrine of the Nicolaitans who taught immortality, immorality and idolatry.

The promise to the overcomers, those who repent and return, is: *"I will give to eat from the tree of life, which is in the midst of the Paradise of God,"* **Verse 7**. The "tree of life" is the tree that was in the Garden of Eden which is now in the city of God in His presence, **Revelation 22:2.** *"Blessed are those who do His commandments, that they may have the right to the tree of life, and may enter through the gates into the city,"* **Revelation 22:14 NKJV**.

Verses 8 - 11

The church at Smyrna: The persecuted church.

Jesus refers to Himself as *"the First and the Last, who was dead, and came to life;"* **Verse 8**. He knows all there is to know from beginning to end, and He is the first to overcome death and the grave. Lack of knowledge, understanding, and what the future holds are worries that the persecuted believer deals with daily. They wonder who will come to their aid, and if they will be able to endure the persecution. The answer is, God is faithful and He has already overcome.

If Jesus calls us, if He equips us, and if He sustains us, then we are in good hands regardless of the opposition. The church at Smyrna appeared to be poor, but they were eternally rich. They were persecuted, slandered, and publicly ridiculed by alleged Jewish leaders, who were servants of Satan. Much like the Jewish leaders were used by Satan at the crucifixion of Jesus, they seemed to be in control, but it was God who was in control, working out His plan of redemption.

These individuals, those opposing the true message of the Gospel and the true followers of Christ Jesus, were about to throw some of the church members into prison. Many had already been thrown into prison and had suffered; but there was a reward not yet received for these sufferings, and that reward was the crown of life rewarded by the hand of Jesus. Temporary suffering is manageable when one knows he will have an "eternal reward" rather than "eternal death." In **James 1:2,** we read: *"My brethren, count it all joy when you fall into various trials, knowing that the testing of your faith produces patience,"* **NKJV**. We also read in **James 1:12** that the crown of life is promised to those who love Jesus.

This testing will quickly come to an end, Jesus says, in *"ten days,"* *Verse* **10**. The conclusion to the ten days is death, but this is not the second death. It is the beginning of eternal life with Christ Jesus in heaven. The encouragement is: *"He who overcomes shall not be hurt by the second death,"* **Verse 11.** In **Revelation 20:14** we read: *"Then Death and Hades were cast into the lake of fire. This is the second death,"* **NKJV.**

Physical death is not to be feared by the followers of Christ Jesus. Eternal death is what ought to be feared. The believer is to trust and obey Jesus. This is what life on earth is all about.

Verses 12 – 17

The church at Pergamos: The compromising church.

Jesus describes Himself as *"He who has the sharp two-edged sword:"* **Verse 12 NKJV.** A two-edged sword cuts both ways, coming and going. A two-edged sword is used in **Hebrews 4:12** as a descriptive term for God's Word, living and powerful, precisely dividing and cutting as in the hand of a surgeon.

God will not tolerate Satan nor anything faintly resembling him. Satan resists God's work, God's Word, and His people. At times believers find themselves surrounded by the forces of Satan, and in those times, it takes great determination to be faithful and trusting to the Word of God. God has a firm grip on His sword but will not unsheathe it until He is ready to unleash His wrath. All things are done in His timing, not ours. The martyr Antipas was a believer who, according to tradition, was roasted in a brazen bowl at the request of the Roman Emperor Domitian, where Satan dwells, or where his power was being visibly displayed.

In spite of their enduring and their suffering in this great persecution, there was a problem. The problem was their failure to deal with idolatry and immorality among their membership. Why? Their failure to expose this great sin among their members had become a stumbling block, an ever-present danger to other believers, both young and old. They were no better than those Nicolaitans, whom Jesus hated, **Verse 6.**

The warning is to turn around or to repent from their condoning of sin by failing to expose it. The result of not repenting of this sin is the unsheathing of God's Sword of His Word upon them. The reward is:

Hidden manna: Heavenly food, nourishment, sustenance. The believer can totally trust God for all that is needed in his life on earth. The children of Israel did not know how the manna got there. All they knew was that God had provided it to sustain them. We do not need to know all about God but we do need to trust His Word.

White stone with a special new name upon it that only he and God knows: A name from the Father to His child, special like none other.

Verses 18 – 29

The church at Thyatira: The corrupt church.

The message to this church is from God who has eyes, John writes, like a flame of fire. Fire is consuming. Fire is understood here to be God's anger. His feet are described as fine brass or polished brass. They are ready to crush in violent judgement or to stamp out these corruptions in the church that anger God.

God's eyes see the good things that this church has done. He sees and acknowledges the love that they expressed to others in and outside the church. He sees the service that they have done and which they are known for outside the church as well. This desire to express love to others and to provide care for those inside and outside the church was an ever-growing ministry. This great love and care was a ministry that they began and was part of their history as a church. It had continued to grow with time. This love seemed to be getting greater and greater, and the eyes of God had witnessed this excellent quality of theirs. They also were patiently working this love and care for others. It was not easy to do, and it required great patience, which they had. But doing good is not the major thing. Loving and obeying God is the major thing.

It is true that Jesus told His disciples that they would be known by their love, the love of God within them. **John 13:35** *"By this all will know that you are My disciples, if you have love one for another,"* **NKJV**. God's love is pure love. It has no aim other than to express the love of God to others for the glory of God and not for personal acknowledgment.

The problem in this church was "tolerance of evil." Specifically, they were tolerating sexual sins in the church. The use of the term *"that woman Jezebel"* is in reference to the queen and wife of King Ahab who considered herself a prophetess of Baal and opponent of Elijah, the true prophet and voice of God, **1 Kings 18 & 19.**

One wonders how this can be tolerated but it was the situation in this church. They did good things but they were corrupt for allowing this sin to grow within the church and also for allowing this teaching to be taught.

The caution to us is to not approve of wrong by our silence. Permitting the mindset of the world to go by without addressing it will corrupt believers and discredit how they serve God. It does not matter what the opinion of society happens to be. The believer has but one authority and guide, which is the Word of God. **James 4:4** *"Adulterers and adulteresses! Do you not know that friendship with the world is enmity with God? Whoever therefore wants to be a friend of the world makes himself an enemy of God,"* **NKJV**.

Notice the patience of God mentioned here in **Verse 21,** *"And I gave her time to repent of her sexual immorality, and she did not repent,"* **NKJV.** God is always patient and kind, even to the worst of society. **2 Peter 3:9:** *"The Lord is not slack concerning His promise, as some count slackness, but is longsuffering toward us, not willing that any should perish but that all should come to repentance,"* **NKJV.**

Even to the worst of sinners, God extends His great love. *"This is a faithful saying and worthy of all acceptance, that Christ Jesus came into the world to save sinners, of whom I am chief,"* **1 Timothy 1:15 NKJV.** Yet, in total disregard to God's great love and His amazing patience, most reject Him.

Jesus tells the reader here that after His patience comes judgment. Be sure to know that no one can fool Jesus for He knows the thoughts and intents of the heart. **Hebrews 4:13** *"And there is no creature hidden from His sight, but all things are naked and open to the eyes of Him to whom we must give account."* **NKJV.**

If a person has Jesus Christ as Lord and Savior, he will be judged at the Judgment Seat of Christ based on the work of Christ Jesus and His righteousness. **2 Corinthians 5:21:** *"For He made Him who knew no sin to be sin for us, that we might become the righteousness of God in Him,* **NKJV.** But for those who do not have Jesus as their Savior, they will be judged by their works. **Revelation 20:12** *"And I saw the dead, small and great, standing before God, and books were opened. And another book was opened, which is the Book of Life. And the dead were judged according to their works, by the things which were written in the books,"* **NKJV.**

The warning here is to those who have not been corrupted or *"as many as do not have this doctrine, who have not known the depths of Satan, as they say, I will put on you no other burden,"* **Revelation 2:24 NKJV**. This teaching of Satan is translated as *"deeper truths"* in the **New Living Translation**.

Be careful of anyone who may claim to have "new truths" or promote "deeper life." Jesus is the Truth and He has given us His truth. Our life is in the depths of Christ Jesus, and the Holy Spirit is our Teacher who teaches us and guides us in all things. Live in Christ Jesus, follow what He has given to us in Scripture, and allow the Holy Spirit to guide. This is available to all believers and for all who seek to live their lives in Christ Jesus.

"But hold fast what you have till I come," **Revelation 2:25 NKJV.** The reward for the overcomer is to reign with Christ Jesus in the 1000-year reign with Him on earth after the Great Tribulation time. Added to this ruling with Christ Jesus is the gift of the *"morning star."* Perhaps the overcomer will be a reflection of the light of Christ Jesus. The overcomer will have that glowing righteousness of Jesus upon him as he rules with Him in this end-time kingdom.

The warning is that the reader must believe what is written to him. He must make the necessary changes in his life as directed by the Holy Spirit.

The caution to us is to live as Scripture teaches, not as society may deem appropriate. God's Word, Scripture, does not change. It is the Truth, and truth does not ever change because it is Truth. Never reason Scripture by the reasoning of society. Judge society by Scripture. He who has an ear, take note.

Chapter 3

Verses 1 – 6

The church at Sardis: The dead church.

The church at Sardis seemed to be a thriving and alive church but that was just a thin coating. This church was as Jesus called the Pharisees of His time on this earth, whitewashed tombs *"which indeed appear beautiful outwardly, but inside are full of dead men's bones and all uncleanness. Even so you also outwardly appear righteous to men, but inside you are full of hypocrisy and lawlessness,"* **Matthew 23:27-28 NKJV**.

In **2 Timothy 3:1-9,** Paul describes those of the last days as being self-serving and hypocritical, who had a form of godliness yet they denied the power of God altogether. *"But know this, that in the last days perilous times will come: For men will be lovers of themselves, lovers of money, boasters, proud, blasphemers, disobedient to parents, unthankful, unholy, unloving, unforgiving, slanderers, without self-control, brutal, despisers of good, traitors, headstrong, haughty, lovers of pleasure rather than lovers of God, having a form of godliness but denying its power. And from such people turn away! For of this sort are those who creep into households and make captives of gullible women loaded down with sins, led away by various lusts, always learning and never able to come to the knowledge of the truth,"* **NKJV**.

I write these comments in June of 2016 while living in Albany, Georgia, and what I see in my present world and in perhaps most churches and with so called Christian leaders of this day is reflective of what Paul writes here. I know things will not get better without a revival and for that revival I earnestly pray.

The church of Sardis of John's day was such a church: *"these things says He who has the seven Spirits,"* **Verse 1**. The "seven Spirits" are the Holy Spirit of God. In **Isaiah 11:2-5,** Isaiah describes the Holy Spirit. The Holy Spirit is our Counselor, our Guide, our Teacher, our Comforter, our Seal of approval and pledge of God, **John 14:15-18; 16:5-15; Ephesians 1:13**. We can also read of the fruit of the Spirit in **Ephesians 5:14-18**.

The "seven stars" are the seven churches which Jesus holds in his hands, **Revelation 1:20**. The Sardis church was out of touch with God though in touch with the world. Being in touch with God is what the believer is asked to strive to do, **James 4:7-8:** *"Therefore submit to God. Resist the devil and he will flee from you. Draw near to God and He will draw near to you. Cleanse your hands, you sinners; and purify your hearts, you double-minded. Lament and mourn and weep! Let your laughter be turned to mourning and your joy to gloom. Humble yourselves in the sight of the Lord, and He will lift you up,"* **NKJV.**

The cure is to be watchful, or to evaluate yourselves with the mirror of the Word of God, and then strengthen the little life that you do have. The situation is critical and the time is short. The church needed revival, a refreshing, and they needed to "remember" what they had been taught. As Paul wrote to the church at Rome in **Romans 13:11-14:** *"And do this, knowing the time, that now it is high time to awake out of sleep; for now our salvation is nearer than when we first believed. The night is far spent, the day is at hand. Therefore let us cast off the works of darkness, and let us put on the armor of light. Let us walk properly, as in the day, not in revelry and drunkenness, not in lewdness and lust, not in strife and envy. But put on the Lord Jesus Christ, and make no provision for the flesh, to fulfill its lusts,"* **NKJV.** Like a thief in the night Jesus will come, unexpected, unannounced, and swift will be His judgment.

God always has a remnant. He has His faithful few, and to the few in Sardis who had remained faithful and not defiled there is a reward. They have proven themselves worthy through the difficult times there in Sardis, and the reward for their faithfulness is that they will rule with Jesus in robes of white at His return. Their names are written in the Book of Life, not blotted out.

The warning is for those who will listen, repent, and obey.

Verses 7 – 13

The church at Philadelphia: The loving and faithful church.

From the hypocritical and dead church, the next letter is to a true, living, loving, and reflector of Christ church, the church at Philadelphia. There were only two churches that did not receive a complaint, and those churches were this church at Philadelphia and the church at Smyrna.

The greeting is from the pure, true and holy God, from God who holds the "key of David," the promised Messiah, King of Kings and Lord of Lords, Jesus, the Messiah and true and proven Ruler of Israel. A key is a symbol of authority, and Jesus told His disciples in **Matthew 28:19** that He was given all "authority" under heaven and earth. The words that are written here are written with authority and were trustworthy, for they were from the hand of the Promised One, the only begotten Son of God, Jesus Christ.

Though the church had opposition, Jesus had "set" before them an open door which He had opened with His authority, and in His authority, it could not be closed by any other. The church at Philadelphia suffered great opposition by those with great power, yet, these powers were helpless in shutting down the work God had placed before them. God's Will **is** to be done. We can count on it.

The work of the church would succeed, though greatly opposed by the power of Satan which would prove to be powerless. The church remained faithful and true while the lie proved to be the lie of Satan. Satan is a liar from the beginning and the father of it. **John 8:44:** *"You are of your father the devil, and the desires of your father you want to do. He was a murderer from the beginning, and does not stand in the truth, because there is no truth in him. When he speaks a lie, he speaks from his own resources, for he is a liar and the father of it,"* **NKJV**.

There is a promise here and that promise is that Jesus will allow them to be preserved or kept *"from the hour of trial which shall come upon the whole world,"* **Verse 10**. Paul told the church at Thessalonica that *"God did not appoint us to wrath, but to obtain salvation through our Lord Jesus Christ,"* **1 Thessalonians 5:9 NKJV**.

What God has prepared for the believer and promised in this letter to the Philadelphia Church is that they would rule with him and worship Him freely in that New Jerusalem, **Revelation 21:22-27**. Jesus tells the church that He is going to give them a new name as well, a family name, perhaps a beloved nick name that will be dear to Jesus, and He will write on the hearts of these His children His new name. The heart of Jesus is expressed to the overcomer with the special loving and new name of Jesus. Be comforted by these words as Jesus encourages the church of brotherly love, Philadelphia.

Verses 14 – 22

The church at Laodicea: The lukewarm church.

The Amen, or the conclusion, the final word, is opening this letter. The characteristics of Jesus are that He is the One who is the Beginning of all and the Conclusion or end of all. He is the Faithful or dependable and true or trusted One.

All things are open and naked before the eyes of the Lord as we read in **Hebrews 4:13:** *"And there is no creature hidden from His sight, but all things are naked and open to the eyes of Him to whom we must give account,"* **NKJV**.

There is nothing that God does not know that can be known, and there was never a time when He did not know all. God is without beginning or end; He is eternal. This is the God who says, *"I know your works,"* **Verse 15**.

This church has no temperature. They are neither hot nor cold, or I could say, they are sickening. Jesus says that He vomits them out of His mouth.

The big problem is that they had been blessed of God by so much that they had come to a point that they felt self-sufficient and had no need of God. How can this be? The believer can do all things "through Christ," **Philippians 4:13,** but he can do nothing without Christ Jesus. Therefore, this church felt that they had no need for the power of God. This sickens God.

The church at Laodicea was a concern to Paul and he wrote about them in his letter to the church at Colosse. **Colossians 4:16:** *"Now when this epistle is read among you, see that it is read also in the church of the Laodiceans, and that you likewise read the epistle from Laodicea,"* **NKJV**.

However, about 30 years later this church is now a sickening church. The church now considers themselves a wealthy church without any desired need. Why? They think they have need of nothing; but in truth, they have need of everything of lasting value. They are described as wretched, miserable, poor, blind, and naked, **Verse 17**.

They are by definition miserable, unhappy, heartbroken, desperate, and in despair. They are hard hearted, difficult to get along with, and uncaring. They don't even realize the truth. They are not looking for a change. They have chosen to remain as they are, dying, despicable, and unlovable.

Jesus offers them a sure remedy: Get your gold from God, get your clothing from God, and get a healing for your eyes from God. Allow God to open your eyes to see clearly. God offers all this to them. He stands at their door knocking for them to open the door, unlike the church at Philadelphia where He has placed before them an open door.

For those who open the door of their hearts, He will give eternal supply, eternal love, and eternal life with Him and the Father. If you have an ear, then listen and obey.

Chapter 4

Verses 1 – 11

Something critical happens in chapter 4. The eyes of John are removed from the churches on earth and are directed to the Throne in Heaven. John writes: *"After these things I looked, and behold, a door standing open in heaven,"* **Verse 1, NKJV.**

Jesus is not knocking at our door. We stand at an open door. The attention of John has been caught because of a voice like a trumpet saying: *"Come up here, and I will show you things which must take place after this,"* **Verse 1.**

John says that he was immediately in the Spirit or Holy Spirit, **Vs. 2.** The Holy Spirit is our Teacher, our Guide, and Seal. Paul writes in **1 Thessalonians 4:16** *"For the Lord Himself will descend from heaven with a shout, with the voice of an archangel and with the trumpet of God. And the dead in Christ will rise first. Then we who are alive and remain shall be caught up together with them in the clouds to meet the Lord in the air. And thus we shall always be with the Lord. Therefore comfort one another with these words."* **NKJV.**

This "caught up" is where we use the word "rapture," or where those whose trust and faith is in Christ Jesus are **raptured** up to heaven, forever to be with the Lord. This is not the Second Coming. Jesus does not place His feet on the Mount of Olives and set up His Millennial Kingdom or the Thousand Year Reign of Christ on the earth.

Now, John finds himself in heaven after being taken there quickly, and he is greatly taken back by what he sees. He sees a throne and someone sitting on the throne glowing with jeweled brilliance. Encircling the throne is a rainbow.

God promise or covenant to Noah to not use a flood to destroy the earth was confirmed by the sight of God's rainbow which He placed in the sky. **Genesis 9:13-17:** *"I set My rainbow in the cloud, and it shall be for the sign of the covenant between Me and the earth. It shall be, when I bring a cloud over the earth, that the rainbow shall be seen in the cloud. And I will remember My covenant which is between Me and you and every living creature of all flesh; the waters shall never again become a flood to destroy all flesh. The rainbow shall be in the cloud, and I will look on it to remember the everlasting covenant between God and every living creature of all flesh that is on the earth. And God said to Noah, 'This is the sign of the covenant which I have established between Me and all flesh that is on the earth.'"* **NKJV.**

Around the throne were 24 smaller thrones and sitting on the smaller thrones were 24 elders. It is widely believed that these 24 "elders" are made up of the 12 apostles and the 12 tribes of Israel. To use the term "widely believed" means that there is no sure understanding as to who they actually are, but they are ruling with the Father.

There are also the "seven fiery lamps" or torches before the throne which are the seven Spirits of God representing the Holy Spirit.

In front of the throne is a sea or space of glowing glass like dazzling crystal. In and about the throne were four living creatures similar to what is described in **Isaiah 6** and **Ezekiel 1 & 10**. The creatures resembled a lion, a calf, a man and an eagle to John. They had six wings full of eyes and were able to see fully with sure perception and not miss anything. They flew day and night, continually praising God with the proclamation: *"Holy, holy, holy, Lord God Almighty, Who was and is and is to come!"* **Verse 8 NKJV.**

With this proclamation comes the response of worship by the 24 elders. They bowed before the throne of God, casting their crowns of glory to the Lord God Almighty. He alone deserves or is worthy of genuine worship. He alone disperses power. He alone is Creator and King. For God's glory all creation has been created to worship God.

What an awesome sight John saw! What an awesome sight we too will see once we receive our reward in heaven. This is beyond my thoughts, or my ability to comprehend, but I will see it. I will witness it one day as will all those who know Jesus Christ as Lord and Savior. He alone is worthy to receive glory and honor and power!

Chapter 5

Verses 1 – 10

The awesome feeling of wonder is suddenly interrupted by what John notices in the right hand of God the Father, which is a scroll. It is worthy to note that the scroll is in the right hand of God the Father in that the right hand is a place of royal significance and importance. The scroll is a document of law or decree, and it is written upon the front and back sides with the royal seal, seven seals in all, John noted.

What does the scroll contain? How will anyone know what is written upon it? The scroll must be opened, and in order to open the scroll the royal seals must be broken. Near the Throne of God, a mighty angel and with a powerful and daunting voice stepped forward and loudly proclaims: *"Who is worthy to open the scroll and to loose its seals?"* **Verse 2**, **NKJV.**

There seemed to be no one to step forward and John began to cry, but one of the elders upon one of the smaller thrones stepped forward to console John and to give him a clearer perception of what was actually happening. There was one worthy and present to take the scroll from the hand of the Father, and he was in the very center of the Throne. It was the all-powerful, all-knowing, ever-present, unchanging Lamb of God, the Lion of Judah, the Root of David or founding Father of the Royal Line of David.

It is interesting that this powerful and worthy authority appeared to be *"a Lamb as though it had been slain,"* **Verse 6**. This is Jesus, the Lamb of God given as a sacrifice for the sins of the world. Jesus told His disciples in **Matthew 28:19** that He was given all authority over all things in the heaven, the earth, and under the earth. Jesus also told His disciples that

He was sending the Holy Spirit who would not speak of Himself but would point men to Him. We see the Holy Spirit described here in **Verse 6**: *"having seven horns and seven eyes, which are the seven Spirits of God sent out into all the earth."*

It is Jesus Himself who was worthy, able, and willing to take the scroll, and He stood up to take the scroll from the hand of the Father.

There was an immediate response to Jesus and that was a great outburst of worship by all who were present. The elders are described as having a harp and a golden bowl of incense. The harp was to accompany the songs of worship and the incense within the bowl was the sweet fragrance of the prayers of the saints that were offered up in praise and worship of God.

2 Corinthians 2:15: *"For we are to God the fragrance of Christ among those who are being saved and among those who are perishing."* **NKJV**

Ephesians 5:2: *"And walk in love, as Christ also has loved us and given Himself for us, an offering and a sacrifice to God for a sweet-smelling aroma."* **NKJV**

Why is Jesus worthy? He was slain for us. He redeemed us to God by His blood. He changed us from sinners to reign with Him as sons and to worship Him as priests.

Verses 11 – 14

Engaged in the worship were thousands and millions of angels, the living beings, and the 24 elders who sang in worship and praise. What was that song? Jesus, the Lamb of God was the focus of the worship. Jesus was worthy to receive honor, glory, and blessing. He was completely and undeniably worthy. He was worthy in power, worthy to be worshiped, worthy by His wisdom, and worthy through His strength.

This is why we worship Jesus today and why we will worship Him forever, because He is worthy. To this worship the 24 elders add their "Amen" or "Yes! It is totally true!" This is what worship in heaven will be like with those who have taken Jesus as their Lord and Savior. This worship will be forever and ever.

Chapter 6

Verses 1 & 2

The First Seal: The White horse and the Conqueror described.

The attention of John is now redirected from what was happening in heaven to what was about to happen on earth. One of the four living creatures before the Throne of God beckons to John, "Come and see." Specifically, John is about to witness God's wrath which was to be poured out during the seven years of Tribulation. We have come from the worship of the Raptured believers in Christ Jesus before His Throne in heaven to those who have been left behind after the Rapture and are awaiting the full wrath of God.

John now is about to witness are those things that will happen in "The Day of The Lord." John has been called up, or raptured, up into heaven before the Throne of God, worshiping with the saints, elders, and angels of heaven. What a wonderful time he has witnessed, but now, what will happen as the seals of the scroll are opened? The warning is for all men to be ready now for that day, as Paul writes: *"Behold, now is the accepted time; behold, now is the day of salvation,"* **2 Corinthians 6:2b NKJV**.

As Jesus, the Lamb, opens the first seal, we see a white horse, a symbol of royalty, and upon the horse is a commander, a victor. This conqueror seems to resemble Christ Jesus, but he is not. Scripture here does not specifically give the identity of the rider of the white horse but he is surely the Antichrist. He is not Christ Jesus but he appears to be like Christ Jesus. Christ Jesus is the one opening the seals. We see that he has a bow, a warrior's weapon, and a crown, a symbol of royal position. There was given to him a royal charge, and he goes out as a warrior, a victor, and a conquer. He goes out upon his white horse conquering as he goes and to conquer all he can. The world is in chaos. The Rapture has happened and millions of people have disappeared. Graves have been opened, and the bodies have disappeared. Many leaders have been taken, loved ones are gone, and whole congregations have disappeared, while other congregations of churches have not been affected. Yes, this Rapture has caused great concern to all who are left behind.

Jesus speaks of this time in **Matthew 24:37-44:** *"But as the days of Noah were, so also will the coming of the Son of Man be. For as in the days before the flood, they were eating and drinking, marrying and giving in marriage, until the day that Noah entered the ark, and did not know until the flood came and took them all away, so also will the coming of the Son of Man be. Then two men will be in the field: one will be taken and the other left. Two women will be grinding at the mill: one will be taken and the other left. Watch therefore, for you do not know what hour your Lord is coming. But know this that if the master of the house had known what hour the thief would come, he would have watched and not allowed his house to be broken into. Therefore you also be ready, for the Son of Man is coming at an hour you do not expect,"* **NKJV.**

We know of several times in Scripture where people have been taken up or raptured away. *"Enoch walked with God; and he was not, for God took him."* This was before the flood and it is recorded in **Genesis 5:24.** Noah, his wife, his three sons, and their wives were taken into the ark and floated above the wrath of the flood. **Genesis 7:1:** *"Then the Lord said to Noah, 'Come into the ark, you and all your household, because I have seen that you are righteous before Me in this generation.' "* **NKJV**. Also we read in **Hebrews 11:7:** *"By faith Noah, being divinely warned of things not yet seen, moved with godly fear, prepared an ark for the saving of his household, by which he condemned the world and became heir of the righteousness* *which is according to faith,"* **NKJV**. **2 Peter 2:5:** *"and did not spare the ancient world, but saved Noah, one of eight people, a preacher of righteousness, bringing in the flood on the world of the ungodly,"* **NKJV**.

Moses, though not taken up, was taken away by God and God alone buried Him, hiding his body from the people. *"So Moses the servant of the Lord died there in the land of Moab, according to the word of the Lord. And He buried him in a valley in the land of Moab, opposite Beth Peor; but no one knows his grave to this day,"* **Deuteronomy 34:5-6 NKJV**. We also read in **Jude 9:** *"Yet Michael the archangel, in contending with the devil, when he disputed about the body of Moses, dared not bring against him a reviling accusation, but said, 'The Lord rebuke you!' "* **NKJV**. Elijah was taken up and only Elisha witnessed it. **2 Kings 2:11-12:** *"Then it happened, as they continued on and talked, that suddenly a chariot of fire appeared with horses of fire, and separated the two of them; and Elijah went up by a whirlwind into heaven. And Elisha saw it, and he cried out, 'My father, my father, the chariot of Israel and its horsemen!' So he saw him no more. And he took hold of his own clothes and tore them into two pieces,"* **NKJV**. And of course, Jesus was taken up into the clouds away from His followers in **Acts 1:9:** *"Now when He had spoken these things, while they watched, He was taken up, and a cloud received Him out of their sight,"* **NKJV**.

Therefore, following the Rapture, there will be a great deal of chaos and uncertainty, and it is into this situation the rider of the white horse goes to gain control of the earth. The Holy Spirit is taken out of the way and the Antichrist is about to be revealed. Paul writes of this time in **2 Thessalonians 2:3-5:** *"Let no one deceive you by any means; for that Day will not come unless the falling away comes first, and the man of sin is revealed, the son of perdition, who opposes and exalts himself above all that is called God or that is worshiped, so that he sits as God in the temple of God, showing himself that he is God. Do you not remember that when I was still with you I told you of* *these things? And now you know what is restraining, that he may be revealed in his own time. For the mystery of lawlessness is already at work; only He who now restrains will do so until He is taken out of the way. And then the lawless one will be revealed, whom the Lord will consume with the breath of His mouth and destroy with the brightness of His coming. The coming of the lawless one is according to the working of Satan, with all power, signs, and lying wonders, and with all unrighteous deception among those who perish, because they did not receive the love of the truth, that they might be saved. And for this reason, God will send them strong delusion, that they should believe the lie, that they all may be condemned who did not believe the truth but had pleasure in unrighteousness,"* **NKJV**.

This is the beginning of that time that is being opened by the Lamb of God, Jesus Christ. The Holy Spirit has been taken out of the way and is no longer restraining Satan's evil work and great lies. So, Satan begins his attempted conquest of the earth and to set up his kingdom, unrestrained, but it will end in defeat by the King of Kings and Lord of Lords, which we read about in **Revelation 19:11-21**.

Did you know that the believer is a conqueror as well right now? We read in **Romans 8:37:** *"Yet in all these things we are more than conquerors through Him who loved us,"* **NKJV**. If God has called you to do something, do it! You cannot fail, you are invincible doing His will. Never question the voice of God. Always go out and do it. Jesus tells all believers to *"go and make disciples,"* **Matthew 28:19 NLT.**

Verses 3 & 4

The Second Seal: Turmoil on the earth.

When the second seal is opened, again John is called to *"Come and see."* John sees a red horse, a horse of great wrath through war. Peace was removed from the earth and everyone was at war with each other. There was no peace on earth, only war. It was the survival of the fittest. Jesus describes such a situation in **Matthew 24: 6-8:** *"And you will hear of wars and rumors of wars. See that you are not troubled: for all these things must come to pass, but the end is not yet. For nation will rise against nation, and kingdom against kingdom. And there will be famines, pestilences, and earthquakes in various places. All these are the beginning of sorrows,"* **NKJV.**

But this time of conflict and war is so much greater. This is like nothing the world has ever seen. This is the Great Tribulation and it is God pouring out His wrath. Be thankful that God has not appointed us to wrath. He has promised to remove us. **1 Thessalonians 5:9 – 11:** *"For God did not appoint us to wrath, but to obtain salvation through our Lord Jesus Christ, who died for us, that whether we wake or sleep, we should live together with Him. Therefore comfort each other and edify one another, just as you also are doing,"* **NKJV**.

Verses 5 & 6

The Third Seal: Commerce on earth is upset.

At the opening of the third seal, John sees a third horse which is black. The rider of the horse has a scale in his hand. The scale is what was used in John's day in commerce to sell and buy things.

There is a great crisis upon the earth and the price of things had soared so high that the cost of a quart of wheat, the desired grain, or three quarts of barley, the less desired grain, sold for a day's wages, although the cost of wine and olive oil were not touched.

In God's economy, He is the provider for us. We read in **Philippians 4:19:** *"And my God shall supply all your need according to His riches in glory by Christ Jesus,"* **NKJV**. God does not forget His children nor is He unaware of their need at any time. We can trust Him though we cannot trust anything else. Place your trust in Him.

Verses 7 & 8

The Fourth Seal: A rampant and great time of death.

The next seal is opened, and John sees a fourth horse. The color of this horse is a pale green. Upon it is a rider, and the name of the rider is Death and Hades. As God moved and scourged the land of Egypt with the death of the first born in the Tenth Plague recorded in **Exodus 12,** the rider, Death and Hades, rides with death in his hand. It is appointed to all men to once die and after this the judgment, as we read in **Hebrews 9:27.**

John is told that one fourth of the earth, 25% of all those alive at that time, would be killed by the sword, or through hunger, disease, and attacks of violent animals on the earth, **Verse 8.**

Verses 9 – 11

The Fifth Seal: The cry of the Martyrs is heard.

With the opening of this fifth seal, John's eyes are directed back to heaven and the altar there. Before God's Throne are all the souls that have been martyred because of their testimony, the message which they faithfully carried in their mission for God on earth. We read of a similar scene in **Revelation 18:24:** *"And in her was found the blood of prophets and saints, and of all who were slain on the earth,"* **NKJV.** This scene followed the fall of Babylon near the conclusion of the Tribulation period. Here in **Verse 9,** John sees these slaughtered martyrs dressed in white robes, and they were expressing with great anguish: *"How long, O Lord, holy and true, until You judge and avenge our blood on those who dwell on the earth?"* **Verse 10 NKJV.**

They are in heaven. They have received the robes of white that Jesus had promised them, yet they still grieved over the timing of God's wrath upon those who had persecuted and slaughtered them, taking their temporal lives. What can we gather from this scene?

They do not have full knowledge in that they express with great anguish, *"How long?"* Today, we who carry the Good News wonder, "How long?" Why would God allow these terrible things to come upon His servants, His messengers who faithfully do that which God has given them to do? Jesus relayed a parable recorded in **Matthew 21:33-46** regarding some wicked servants who had killed the messengers that the owner of the vineyard had sent to the servants, or vinedressers of that vineyard, and also his son. Jesus asked the chief priests and elders of the people, *"What will he do to these vinedressers?"* The response was: *"He will destroy those wicked men miserably,"* **NKJV**.

Here is the truth: God will destroy miserably but it will be in His timing, not in our impatient and short-tempered timing. God is long-suffering and He is patient. He is tempered because He wants everyone, even the vilest of men, to have all the time necessary for them to make a clear decision to repent and be saved or to reject totally His precious Son. Peter writes in **2 Peter 3:9**, *"The Lord is not slack concerning His promise, as some count slackness, but is longsuffering toward us, not willing that any should perish but that all should come to repentance,"* **NKJV**.

God, in His great wisdom and power created this world, and it is with that same great wisdom and power that He will destroy all that reject Him. He is not swayed by the thoughts of His creation nor does He seek any advice. God plans and He works His plan just as He planned it.

We read in **Verse 11**: *"rest a little while longer,"* or as we might tell our impatient children, "Just hold your horses; it's not time yet." The rest of the verse makes known to the martyrs as well as to the reader that many more will be slaughtered and killed for the cause of the Gospel. The writer of Hebrews writes in **Hebrews 11:38**: *"of whom the world was not worthy. They wandered in deserts and mountains, in dens and caves of the earth. And all these, having obtained a good testimony through faith, did not receive the promise, God having provided something better for us, that they should not be made perfect apart from us,"* **NKJV.**

God is waiting for the last martyr to be slain and when that occurs He will unleash His judgment with great power. Randy Alcorn, in his novel, Safely Home, describes such a scene:

"How Long, O Lord?" the voices of millions cried out.

"Because of the oppression of the weak and the groaning of the needy, I will now arise," said the King. "I will rescue them."

The King stood in front of his throne. His eyes—and all those across the heavens—were fixed now on a young locksmith from Pushan, (the main character soon to be martyred, the last martyr) *who languished in prison, dying of tuberculosis, coughing up blood. As Li Shen's life faded, the King gripped the hilt of the sword, then unsheathed it. He lifted it up, stretching out his arm. He whistled to a white stallion, a creature unlike any other. It flew to him, dancing and snorting, rising up on its back legs, eager to run to battle. The King, shining with the brilliance of a thousand quasars, mounted his great steed.*

All Heaven watched the young man breathe his last at the feet of his tormentors. At that moment the Warrior-King, eyes wet and white-hot, cried out with a voice that shook heaven and earth: "No longer!"

Michael threw his arm forward, the hosts of heaven shouted, and millions of horses gathered, mounted by warriors of every tribe, nation, and tongue. Eternity's door swung open on its   hinges. Out of one realm and into another rode an army like there had never been.

"The time has come," roared the King. "Rescue my people! Destroy my enemies!" The Morning Star, who had once come as Lamb, now returned as Lion, with ten thousand galaxies forming the train of his imperial robe." **Randy Alcorn – <u>Safely Home</u>**.

This is awesome, but it falls short in describing the actual event, *"until both the number of their fellow servants and their brethren, who would be killed as they were, was accomplished,"* **Verse 11b.**

Verses 12 – 17

The Sixth Seal: The day of wrath comes with cosmic upheaval.

John's eyes are returned to the earth and there he witnesses the Lamb opening the sixth seal. With the opening of the sixth seal is a great earthquake such as the earth has never experienced before. The smoke from this great earthquake hid the view of the sun and the moon seemed to be a blood red reflection of God's power.

Stars fell from the sky like the over-ripened fruit of a tree being shook by a great windstorm in autumn. **Jude** writes of this time in **Verses 14b & 15 NKJV,** *"Behold, the Lord comes with ten thousands of His saints, to execute judgment on all, to convict all who are ungodly among them of all their ungodly deeds which they have committed in an ungodly way, and of all the harsh things which ungodly sinners have spoken against Him."* Peter also describes this time in **2 Peter 3:10:** *"But the day of the Lord will come as a thief in the night, in which the* *heavens will pass away with a great noise, and the elements will melt with fervent heat; both the earth and the works that are in it will be burned up."* **NKJV.**

Who, indeed will be able to stand? Place your trust in God, receive His gift of Salvation, take His Son, Jesus Christ as your Savior, and He will deliver you. He came as the Sacrificial Lamb the first time, and the next time He will come as Judge. These things are difficult to comprehend but there is yet another seal to be opened by the Lamb of God.

Chapter 7

Verses 1 – 8

The interlude to the opening of the Seventh Seal: The sealing of the 144,000 prophets of God, His messengers.

Like the calm before a storm, we read of a great stillness with no wind blowing, not a leaf in the tree is moving, the sea is calm, and is as clear as glass. There is an angel that makes an appearance before John and he has a seal in his hand which gives him authority from the living God. The announcement is that the four angels, from the four corners of the earth who have the power to unleash great wrath upon the earth, its vegetation and the sea, are to hold back the wrath that they have been given, until God places His seal upon them. They would be proclaiming the Word of God as His servants to those who are on the earth during these days of Great Tribulation. The seal of God is the seal of authority and protection from God.

The number of those servants is 144,000. There are 12,000 from each of the 12 tribes of Israel. There are two tribes that are not represented here, and they are the tribe of Dan and the tribe of Ephraim. These two tribes are replaced by Joseph and Levi. Perhaps the tribe of Dan was left out because of their great idolatry as recorded in **Judges 17** and **18**. One can only speculate. The bottom line is that the twelve tribes represented are those that God chose. We do not need to know the mind of God because we cannot know it nor can we know it, for we are mere creatures, beings, and God is the Creator.

The seal of God guarantees that they will be able to stand through the Tribulation. The final statement of **Chapter 6, Verse 17** is a question: *"For the great day of His wrath has come, and who is able to stand?"* **NKJV.** The answer is: Those who have the seal of God upon their head and those who refuse the number of the Beast recorded in **Chapter 13:16-18,** *"He causes all, both small and great, rich and poor, free and slave, to receive a mark on their right hand or on their foreheads, and that no one may buy or sell except one who has the mark or the name of the beast or the number of his name. Here is wisdom. Let him who has understanding calculate the number of the beast, for it is the number of a man: His number is 666,"* **NKJV.** We see these 144,000 servants again in **Chapter 14:1-5**. They made it through. They were able to stand.

Verses 9 -17

John witnessed another group with the 144,000, and it was without number. This group was from all over the earth. They were from every tribe, every section of the earth, from all languages, and from all people groups. They were standing in heaven before the Throne of God worshiping God. These people were praising God for deliverance, reward, and salvation. The lyrics of their song were referring to His salvation which is a complete salvation, eternal salvation. The worship was directed to an audience of One, the Lamb who sits on the Throne, to Him alone, He who was worthy to take the scroll and unseal it. All of heaven joined in as they sang:

"Amen! Blessing and glory and wisdom,

Thanksgiving and honor and power and might,

Be to our God forever and ever.

*Amen. (**Revelation 7:12 NKJV**)*

It is odd that one of the elders asks John to identify the crowd, perhaps to make a point. John's answer is followed by, *"Sir, you know."* **Verse 14, NKJV.** The elder says, "Yes! These are those who have come out of great tribulation, and who have been washed in the blood of the Lamb of God, and who have washed their robes in the blood of the Lamb. They have been made as white as the fresh blown snow." **(My paraphrase of Verse 14)**

God recognizes them and cares for them both day and night for ever and ever. We read in **Verses 16-17:** *"They shall neither hunger anymore nor thirst anymore; the sun shall not strike them, nor any heat; for the Lamb who is in the midst of the throne will shepherd them and lead them to living fountains of waters. And God will wipe away every tear from their eyes."* **NKJV.**

This is a comforting thought and reminder that Jesus is our Great Shepherd who cares for His sheep, but what is about to happen will cause great fear with the opening of the seventh seal, containing the seven trumpets, and the wrath they are about to sound forth.

Chapter 8

Verse 1

The Seventh Seal: The Seven Trumpets are announced.

With the opening of the seventh seal of the scroll comes the appearance of seven angels, each holding a trumpet. The blowing of a trumpet is a signal for an announcement or action to begin and in this instance, it is a battle cry or signal for the long-awaited judgment of God upon evil. The opening of this seventh seal is preceded by a great hush in heaven. John writes that the silence lasts for about a half hour. They wait for the opening of the seventh and final seal of the scroll in silence. We read in **Zephaniah 1:7** *"Be silent in the presence of the Lord God; for the day of the Lord is at hand, for the Lord has prepared a sacrifice; He has invited His guests,"* **NKJV**. John is the invited guest to witness the announcement of God's ever-increasing wrath upon the earth in this great Day of Judgment upon the earth.

The censor was used as prayers were offered in the temple, and here the many prayers of the saints before the altar of the Lord are about to be answered. There have been many prayers and the angel was given much incense, a sweet savor of answered prayer rising up to the very Throne of God. Be sure to know that all prayers are always answered by God at the best time, the right time, and the most effective time. Never feel that your prayers go unheard, servant of God. God knows our need even before we ask and has prepared the best answer to each prayer. All prayers are answered personally by God on behalf of the one offering the prayer.

As the angel throws the flaming censor to the earth, the prayers of the saints are being answered. "How long?" has been the prayer of the saints throughout time, and we hear it expressed here, even before the Throne. The answer to those prayers has come and the answer is, "right now." The effect of the flaming censor being cast to the earth is great noise, thunder, and lighting. Now the angels lift their trumpets, ready to sound their message of judgment.

Verse 7

The First Trumpet: Vegetation is struck.

With the sounding of the first trumpet, hail and fire ravaged the earth, and there were many who died or were killed in this hail and fire storm. One third of all plant life was burned up.

Verses 8 & 9

The Second Trumpet: The Sea is struck.

Quickly following the first trumpet and its destruction comes the second trumpet. At the sounding of the second trumpet, John says that he sees "something like a great mountain," perhaps a huge meteor or something prepared by God for just this event. God prepared a great fish to swallow Jonah, **Jonah 1:17:** *"Now the Lord had prepared a great fish to swallow Jonah. And Jonah was in the belly of the fish three days and three nights."* **NKJV**

This, "something like a great mountain," affected a third of the seas, or the bodies of salt water upon the earth, and those waters became like blood, killing a third of all the fish of the salt water seas as well as destroying one third of all the ships that were sailing upon the seas.

Verses 10 & 11

The Third Trumpet: The fresh water rivers, lakes, reservoirs, and streams destroyed.

Again, a great "star," perhaps a meteorite which is aflame, fell upon the fresh springs of drinking water of the earth and polluted them. This bitterness was as Wormwood and many people died from drinking the bitter waters.

Verses 12 & 13

The Fourth Trumpet: The heavens, the universe, is struck.

Quickly following the blowing of the third trumpet and the destruction, the blowing of the fourth trumpet is heard. The sun, moon, and stars are blotted out or the light from them is hidden or unobservable to the human eye, perhaps an effect of what has already happened.

If the warmth of the sun is hindered, there would be a lowering of the natural or ordinary temperature of the earth. One third of the day, or eight hours of normal day light, and one third of the night, or eight hours of the night which would normally be lit by the moon and where stars and planets could be normally observed, were blotted out or darkened. That means that light could only be noticed for eight hours of the day.

Chapter 9

Verses 1 – 12

The Fifth Trumpet: Locusts from the Bottomless Pit, the first of **The Three Woes.**

The fifth, sixth, and the seventh trumpets also contain **The Three Woes.** From the blowing of this fifth trumpet, all hell is released, perhaps one might say. What has happened thus far is terrible, but now God sends and angel, a star falls from heaven, John writes, and this angel has in his hand the key to the "bottomless pit," the abyss. We see this angel again in **Revelation 20:1:** *"Then I saw an angel coming down from heaven, having the key to the bottomless pit and a great chain in his hand,"* **NKJV. Jude** also make mention of the bottomless pit when he writes in **Verse 6:** *"And the angels who did not keep their proper domain, but left their own abode, He has reserved in everlasting chains under darkness for the judgment of the great day;"* **NKJV**.

It is these fallen angels whoS are now released by the angel from Heaven. With the opening of the pit bellows a great smoke affecting the air to be breathed and further hiding the light of the sun. What seems to be locust creatures rush up out of the pit and they were given power over mankind for a select timing of five months (**Verse 5**). These creatures resembled war horses eager for battle. Though reminding John of a horse, their faces were as the face of a man with long hair, and they had a golden crown upon their head. Perhaps the crown is representative of the authority that they have been given. They had large teeth, a warrior's breastplate, and wings that created a fearsome sound like horses going into battle. Their offensive weapon, apparently, was the scorpion-like tail they had to inflict great pain upon their prey.

Their rampage is not that of normal locusts which would destroy all vegetation. They were prevented from touching the vegetation. God had already destroyed one third of all vegetation after the first trumpet.

The wrath that these inhabitants of the bottomless pit bring was to be focused upon all those who did not have the seal of God upon their foreheads. The torment that these creatures caused would not cause death but was a torture that was like the sting of a scorpion upon its prey. The pain is so great that people would try to commit suicide, but they would not be able to take their own lives. Whatever they might do to end their lives would fail. For five months, these creatures would torture the select group of mankind. These were five long months, almost a year.

Their leader is Abaddon, in Greek Apollyon, who is the Destroyer or Satan. Satan revels in the great destruction that these warriors would bring about. There are two more woes and trumpets that are yet to come from the opening of the seven seals of the scroll.

Verses 13 – 21

The Sixth Trumpet and Second Woe: The captive angels of the Euphrates released.

John is describing for the reader something that he has never seen before and uses things that he has seen to describe that which he has never seen. He uses this tactic throughout his writing of Revelation. The command from heaven given to the sixth angelic trumpeter in **Verses 13 – 14** is for the release of four angels from the Euphrates River who had been specifically prepared for this specific moment in time. They are from the pit of the bottomless pit. The door for these evil angels is around the Euphrates River. They have at their command a mighty army like no other consisting of

200,000,000. Now that number is unheard of but John adds, *"I heard the number of them."* **Verse 16 NKJV.**

John perhaps is saying: I didn't count them but I clearly heard the number spoken. He describes his vision of this 200,000,000 army as being on horseback. It is a cavalry of warriors. They are fearsome creatures in sight, sound, and mission. The warrior's protective armor and uniform was a breastplate which was colored in red, blue, and yellow.

John describes these war horses is this manner: The head of these horses resembled the head of a lion, with thick mane, and out of their mouth came fire, smoke and brimstone. We read a similar description of the pit in **Revelation 21:8:** *"But the cowardly, unbelieving, abominable, murderers, sexually immoral, sorcerers, idolaters, and all liars shall have their part in the lake which burns with fire and brimstone, which is the second death."* **NKJV.**

John notes that they came from the east on their way to Armageddon (**Revelation 16:12**). The destructive power in which these horses caused harm and death was in their mouth and their tail and in the three plagues that they carried in the fire, smoke, and brimstone. We might say, "They destroyed everything, coming and going," but their power came from their vicious mouth and the sting or poisonous snake-like bite of their tail.

The death total mounted to one third of mankind. **Verse 18:** *"By these three plagues a third of mankind was killed—by the fire and the smoke and the brimstone which came out of their mouths,"* **NKJV.** The events of which the Seven Trumpet Angels heralded will take place in the first half of the Tribulation and with these events the Antichrist, or Beast, with the power of Satan were used to set up Satan's rule.

With all the wrath of God contained in the first six seals with their six trumpets and two woes, it made little or no impact upon those under the grip of Satan. We read in **Verses 20 & 21:** *"But the rest of mankind, who were not killed by these plagues, did not repent of the works of their hands, that they should not worship demons, and idols of gold, silver, brass, stone, and wood, which can neither see nor hear nor walk. And they did not repent of their murders or their sorceries or their sexual immorality or their thefts."* **NKJV.**

Jesus says of these times in **Matthew 24:21-22:** *"For then there will be great tribulation, such as has not been since the beginning of the world until this time, no, nor ever shall be. And unless those days were shortened, no flesh would be saved; but for the elect's sake those days will be shortened,"* **NKJV.** Jesus is saying that if the length of this Great Tribulation had been any longer, even the 144,000 prophets would be destroyed. But that is not what God will do. God never allows anything or does anything that would go against His predetermined will. God works all things out for His glory and His children's good. **Romans 8:28:** *"And we know that all things work together for good to those who love God, to those who are the called according to His purpose."* **NKJV**

Can I explain clearly all these things? No, and neither can anyone else. They are a mystery. They are the things that God showed John, and he described them under the inspiration of the Holy Spirit. We accept them by faith. Many people relate these creatures to things that we know today, but these are creatures that God has prepared for that specific time, just as he prepared the fish for Jonah. We are no more able to understand mysterious things that are written in the book of **Revelation** than John. Those things, those creatures that John strained to describe, are just as much a mystery today. Therefore, we need not seek to understand everything, but we need to believe everything contained in Scripture. We do not need to clearly know; we need only to clearly see Jesus, the Author and Finisher of our faith. We can believe Scripture now with the promise and assurance that one day we will see and understand clearly. Never allow yourself to become dogmatic on things that are uncertain. Believe God's Word, the Scriptures, based solely upon and leaning upon the Holy Spirit for your understanding and learning. Never place the thoughts of another human being, a creation of God, above what is not written in Scripture. There are things that only God knows. Seek the wisdom, knowledge and understanding that the Holy Spirit gives us, teaches us, and reminds us. We read in **1 Corinthians 13:12**: *"For now we see in a mirror, dimly, but then face to face. Now I know in part, but then I shall know just as I also am known."* **NKJV.**

Chapter 10

Verses 1 – 7

The mighty angel with the little book.

After these things, John sees something else which is a mighty angel. Seeing an angel caused confusion and fear but a "mighty angel" is what John sees here. What is it about this angel that would cause John to refer to him as a mighty angel? He is wrapped in a cloud, there is a glowing rainbow upon his head, and his face is difficult to see in that it glowed with the brightness of the sun, and from his feet bellowed flames of fire. This will certainly get one's attention!

The angel had something in his hand, and that was a small book which was open, perhaps a scroll that was unrolled. This book, scroll, or document was a royal edict. The angel spoke with authority and power. He stood with his feet firmly planted upon the land and the seas and his hand raised to heaven. With a loud and powerful voice, he began to speak, and his voice quickly prompted seven extremely loud voices, like the sound of thunder. The seven united voices had a single message which they loudly proclaimed. As John was about to record what the seven thunders proclaimed, a voice quickly came from heaven with the command for John not to record what the seven thunders proclaimed.

The mighty angel then began to proclaim the message which was given to him. With his hand raised to heaven and under oath, he stated that God's wrath has officially begun. There would not be any further delay in that wrath. He affirms that with the sounding of the seventh angel's trumpet will be the fulfilling of God's mysterious will, just as God had promised.

Nothing deters God's will, or God's plan, because God's will is done on earth just as it is in heaven, as we were taught to pray in the model prayer in **Matthew 6:10**.

Verses 8 – 11

The little book is eaten.

John is told to take the little book which the angel has and eat it. He is told that it will taste sweet but will be bitter in his stomach, and as my grandparents might say, "It won't set well with you." What John is about to reveal is sweet as far as the fulfilling of God's plan, but it is quite upsetting as it is set into action. The bitter effect of God's wrath will be unleashed upon almost every person of every nation and every language, both rich and poor.

Chapter 11

Verses 1 & 2

The Measuring of the Temple.

John now is told to measure the new Temple which has been rebuilt. Just the acknowledgment that the Temple has been rebuilt brings to my mind that at the present time, which is June of 2017, upon the Temple mount there is the Muslim Dome of the Rock, which has been there since 691 A.D., and also built there is the Masjid al-Aqsa mosque, which is supposed to be where Muhammad was transported from Masjid al-Haram to Masjid al-Mosque and Muhammad's supposed ascension to heaven.

These two structures are no longer there. What happened? There is only speculation but the Antichrist is making his move in this Great Tribulation time. Times are bad but they are about to get much worse.

John is given a reed or a measuring stick to measure the Temple and the altar there, excluding the Court of the Gentiles. Maybe this is referring to the Muslims. They are presently treading underfoot that holy place; but here the Gentiles will be desecrating the holy place for forty-two months, or three and a half years of the Tribulation.

Verses 3 – 6

The Two Witnesses revealed.

During the first three and a half years of the Tribulation, along with the 144,000 prophets of God will be two powerful witnesses. They have been empowered with the protection of God as they proclaim God's message of repentance and soon coming judgment. This is the mission which God will give them.

For three and a half years they will powerfully proclaim God's message and, in so doing, irritate the Antichrist and his followers. They are called "two olive trees and two lampstands," or perhaps I could say, they are the anointed voice of God making known or holding up the light of God's Word to the condemned.

These Two Witnesses have the power to call down fire from heaven as God's wrath upon those who might desire to harm them. They can also shut up heaven or restrict rain from watering the earth. They can bring plagues upon anyone that they wish. These Two Witnesses remind us of the feats of Elijah and Moses, which is who they are.

Though they have this power, they still clothe themselves in sackcloth and ashes, for their message is of wrath upon all unrepentant men. The world has been tormented by the daily message of the Two Witnesses.

Verses 7 - 10

The conclusion of their mission.

John writes in **Verse 7** that after their mission had been completed, they are killed by the Antichrist. This was not a victory of the Antichrist, it was the conclusion of the Two Witnesses' mission.

This tells believers that they are invincible while doing what God has called them to do. God's will, will always be done completely. It is only when we act outside of God's will and His plan that we can fail.

After the death of the Two Witnesses, the people from all around the earth party and celebrate. Perhaps the scene is televised. The horrific sight is celebrated by unbelievers everywhere. As the bodies of the Two Witnesses begin to decay over the next three and a half days in the streets of Jerusalem, the city where Jesus was crucified, something astonishing happens. Amidst all the celebration and in their mistaken sense of victory, suddenly the breath of life comes upon the decaying bodies of the Two Witnesses, and they stand fully alive. The celebration stops and there is heard an undeniable voice from heaven saying, *"Come up here,"* **Verse 12**. With that invitation, the Two Witnesses, Elijah and Moses, ascend through the clouds and into heaven. Accompanied with this ascension is a great earthquake in Jerusalem. It destroys a tenth of the city, and seven thousand people die.

The celebration turns to great fear and then to glory being given to God. As the rocks would cry out so, too, these rock-hardened deniers of God give praise to God; but this praise will not last. This is not a genuine repentance by most but is a response out of their great fear, although perhaps there are large numbers saved. There will be those who would turn to God during the Tribulation and then go with the 144,000 Prophets into the Millennial Reign of Christ after His Second Coming. This is common to see today: a short acknowledgment of God, seeking help from God, and a glorifying of God in times of tragedy; but it rarely lasts.

Following all this quickly comes the Seventh Trumpet and the Third Woe.

Verses 15 – 19

The Seventh Trumpet: God's Kingdom proclaimed.

Now comes the announcement and sounding of the Seventh Trumpet and the Third Woe. The beginning of the end is proclaimed and John begins by defining the characters that will carry out these last three and a half years of the Great Tribulation. John uses figurative form to relay these. He begins by allowing us to have a glimpse of God's New Kingdom and His victory over the kingdoms of this present world. What we see is something like an "open house" display of heaven.

The announcement is followed with great rejoicing in heaven, and the twenty-four elders worship God for what is about to take place. They begin in **Verse 17** by saying, *"We give You thanks, O Lord God Almighty."* In heaven and in the opening of the Temple of God, John sees the Ark of the Covenant displayed in the Temple in this preview opening of heaven. Accompanied with this preview is a divine light show with great noise, thunder, hail and a great shaking of the earth, or an earthquake.

Chapter 12

The characters involved in this chapter and in Chapter 13 are in figurative form, and they are:

- **Israel:** The woman with child, God's chosen people who exemplify mankind's unfaithfulness and through whom God displays His patience, faithfulness, and love to all mankind's unfaithfulness, bent to sin, and who need a Savior.
- **Satan:** Cast out of heaven, opposes God, and accuses men of sin.
- **Jesus:** The Only Begotten Son of God, sent to earth to redeem the world of sin.
- **The Antichrist:** The first Beast. He does and carries out the will of Satan.
- **The False Prophet:** The second Beast, directs men to the Antichrist.
- **The Unholy Trinity:**
  - o **Satan:** The false Father
  - o **Antichrist**: Doing the will of his father Satan. The false Christ.
  - o **False Prophet**: The false Holy Spirit. He Points mankind to the Antichrist.

Thus far we have witnessed the wrath of God being poured out upon the earth and its inhabitants. The 144,000 prophets of God have been charged, empowered, and given God's protective hand as they do what God has given them to do. This has happened during the first three and a half years of the Great Tribulation. Now we will begin to see God step back as He allows Satan, along with his Antichrist and false prophet, to unleash his power upon the remaining people on the earth and his wrath upon the followers of God.

Verses 1 – 6

Israel and Satan's wrath upon them.

Here, we first see a description of the chosen people of God, Israel. It is through the people of Israel that God chose to send His Only Begotten Son, Jesus, in an Immaculate Conception. Israel was God's chosen people and Mary was God's chosen vessel to bring Jesus into this world. She carried the sinful seed of mankind and the Holy Spirit carried the divine seed of God, who cannot sin.

So, Jesus came into this world as a baby whose mother was human, with the seed of sin in her, and therefore, Jesus was born into sin, or with the seed of sin in Him. This was one needed factor for God the Father to forgive mankind's sin. Mary was a descendent of King David, making Jesus born in the lineage and heritage of King David which was needed for Him to be the fulfillment of prophecy to be a true heir to the Throne of David.

These elements must be true of Jesus for Him to be the true and pure sacrifice for sin. It was necessary for Jesus to be born of man and born of God, the son of man and Son of God. All these things had to be true for God to rightfully forgive sin.

These elements were necessary for Jesus, God's Son, to be tempted in all points as we are but without sin. Jesus had to take on the image of man to have a heritage of sinful man. Mary provided that in the birth of Jesus and the Holy Spirit provided the God part. **Hebrews 4:15:** *"For we do not have a Hight Priest who cannot sympathize with our weaknesses, but was in all points tempted as we are, yet without sin."* **NKJV.**

There is another factor which was that Jesus must be sinless in His living on earth. The only way Jesus could have the ability not to sin was to have the sinless attribute of God, by having no earthly father but a divine and sinless one, and the Holy Spirit provided that part. **Luke 1:34-35:** *"Then Mary said to the angel, 'How can this be, since I do not know a man?' And the angel answered and said to her, 'The Holy Spirit will come upon you, and the power of the Highest will overshadow you; therefore, also, that Holy One who is to be born will be called the Son of God.' "* **NJKV.** So, Jesus was son of man and Son of God. This was the only way; it was God's way. This needed to be true in order for God to forgive sin. *"To sin is human, to forgive is divine,"* or as more correctly quoted, *"To err is human, to forgive divine,"* by Alexander Pope.

Jesus was the Only Begotten Son of the Father. The Holy Spirit proceeds from the Father and does not speak of Himself but points all men to Jesus. **John 16:13 & 14:** *"However, when He, the Spirit of truth, has come, He will guide you into all truth; for He will not speak on His own authority, but whatever He hears He will speak; and He will tell you things to come. He will glorify Me, for He will take of what is Mine and declare it to you."* **NKJV.**

So, Israel is represented here as *"a woman clothed with the sun, with the moon under her feet, and on her head a garland of twelve stars."* **Verse 1, NKJV.** Jesus is the light of the world, and Israel and all believers are a reflector of His light to the world. Israel, the woman, is the one through whom the Savior came. Israel was and is protected by God for she is His chosen people. One of these events is recorded in **Matthew 2:16:** *"Then Herod, when he saw that he was deceived by the wise men, was exceedingly angry; and he sent forth and put to death all the male children who were in Bethlehem and in all its districts, from two years old and under, according to the time which he had determined from the wise men,"* **NKJV.** The twelve stars are the twelve tribes of Israel. God protects her from being destroyed by Satan, the *"great, fiery red dragon having seven heads and ten horns, and seven diadems on his heads."* **Verse 3, NKJV**.

In **Verses 3 & 4,** we read of Satan being cast out of heaven and with him one third of the created angels. We also read of Satan's rebellion in **2 Peter 2:4,** *"For if God did not spare the angels who sinned, but cast them down to hell and delivered them into chains of darkness, to be reserved for judgment;"* and in **Ezekiel 28:12-15,** *"You were the seal of perfection, Full of wisdom and perfect in beauty. You were in Eden the garden of God; Every precious stone was your covering . . . you were the anointed cherub who covers; I established you; You were on the holy mountain of God; You walked back and forth in the midst of fiery stones. You were perfect in your ways from the day you were created, till iniquity was found in you,"* **NKJV**. Isaiah also tells of Satan's fall in **Isaiah 14:12-21,** *"How you are fallen from heaven, O Lucifer, son of the morning! How are you cut down to the ground, you who weakened the nations! For you have said in your heart: 'I will ascend into heaven, I will exalt my throne above the stars of God; I will also sit on the mount of the congregation on the farthest side of the north; I will ascend above the heights of the clouds, I will be like the Most High.' Yet you shall be brought down to Sheol, to the lowest depths of the Pit . . . ."* **NKJV**.

Satan continues to resist God and lie. He was a liar from the beginning, as Jesus says in **John 8:44,** *"You are of your father the devil, and the desires of your father you want to do. He was a murderer from the beginning, and does not stand in the truth, because there is no truth in him. When he speaks a lie, he speaks from his own resources for he is a liar and the father of it."* **NKJV**.

This is the accuser of the brethren that we read about in **Verses 10-12:** *"Then I heard a loud voice saying in heaven, 'Now salvation, and strength, and the kingdom of our God, and* the power of His Christ have come, for the accuser of our brethren, who accused them before our God day and night, has been cast down. And they overcame him by the blood of the Lamb and by the word of their testimony, and they did not love their lives to the death. Therefore rejoice, O heavens, and you who dwell in them! Woe to the inhabitants of the earth and the sea! For the devil has come down to you, having great wrath, because he knows that he has a short time.' " **NKJV**.

"He knows that he has a short time." This is a terrible woe in that we know Satan is not held back in using all he has to inflict pain, suffering, and his wrath upon those alive at this time on the earth. Yes, this is a great and terrible thing! "Woe to the inhabitants of the earth and the sea!" **Verse 12**

Verses 13 – 17

Satan wreaks havoc upon the Jewish nation in these last three and a half years but they have God to give them an escape. God always makes a way of escape. No one can prevent God's protective hand from being used as He desires. God is Supreme, no exception, ever!

"And the dragon was enraged with the woman, and he went to make war with the rest of her offspring, who keep the commandments of God and have the testimony of Jesus Christ," Verse **17 NKJV**. Satan is enraged because he knows his time is short, but he does not know the exact time; only God does, so Satan continues on. He knows the clock is running out but cannot see the clock.

What a fearful time! I am glad that the believer will not have to experience such wrath. God has not appointed us to wrath. **1 Thessalonians 5:9:** "For God did not appoint us to wrath, but to obtain salvation through our Lord Jesus Christ . . . Therefore comfort each other and edify one another, just as you are doing." **NKJV**.

Chapter 13

Verses 1 – 9

The appearance of the Antichrist.

As John stands upon the seashore, he sees a Beast arising from the sea, perhaps the pit of hell. The Beast is the Antichrist. He rises with a mission and that mission is to set up a kingdom for Satan. His purpose is to do the will of Satan and oppose the will of God.

The Beast seems to remind John of a leopard, with feet like a bear and having seven heads with ten horns. Each horn had a crown upon it. The mouth of the Beast reminded John of that of a lion. The Beast had great power, but it was not his power. It was power that was given to him by Satan.

All of this is symbolism. It is a picture of what the Antichrist is all about and what he will do. The leopard is swift, the bear is powerful, and the lion is all consuming. The Antichrist will move quickly, powerfully, and with unrelenting wrath to do the will of him who sent him—the dragon, the old serpent, the devil or Satan.

The seven heads are a false representation of the seven Spirits of God, which we have witnessed before the throne of God in heaven in **Revelation 4:5:** *"And from the throne proceeded lightings, thunderings, and voices. Seven lamps of fire were burning before the throne, which are the seven Spirits of God."* **NKJV**.

Each of the seven heads has a blasphemous name upon it, or a name that dishonors God. A horn is symbolic of national power. The ten horns represent the ten nations that will govern with the Antichrist to help advance his mission in these last three and a half years of the Great Tribulation.

One of the seven heads on the Beast, the Antichrist, has a mortal wound that has been healed by Satan and because of that false resurrection, the world followed the leadership of the Beast and lauded Satan and worshipped Satan as God for what they witnessed, **Verses 4 - 8:** *"So they worshipped the dragon who gave authority to the beast; and they worshipped the beast, saying, 'Who is like the beast? Who is able to make war with him?' And he was given a mouth speaking great things and blasphemies, and he was given authority to continue for forty-two months. Then he opened his mouth in blasphemy against God, to blaspheme His name, His tabernacle, and those who dwell in heaven. It was granted to him to make war with the saints and to overcome them. And authority was given him over every tribe, tongue, and nation. All who dwell on the earth will worship him, whose names have not been written in the Book of Life of the Lamb slain from the foundation of the world."* **NKJV**.

John gives a warning that he heard from his vision, and that was one of caution. If you have an ear use it. Take the necessary actions to prevent your being part of this event of the Great Tribulation. Let the reader take warning, perhaps I might say.

Satan, the Antichrist, the false prophet, and all their captive followers and all who carry out this wrath of Satan will experience eternal death. Yet, those whose names are written in the Lamb's Book of Life will be given eternal life. Those who endure will receive their reward from God Almighty. Satan and all who are with him will be judged very soon.

Verses 11 – 18

We now are introduced to the third part of the "unholy trinity," which is the False Prophet who helps the Antichrist and is a false representation of the Holy Spirit of God. The False Prophet promotes the Antichrist and works alongside him.

This second Beast is seen as coming up out of the earth. This second Beast seemed to have two horns that resemble the horns of a lamb, yet had the voice of a dragon. He had authority and spoke with the authority of the dragon, Satan.

The False Prophet used the power that he had to make all on the earth worship the Antichrist, or the first Beast. Satan had given him authority as well to do false signs, wonders, and miracles, much like the Pharaoh's Egyptian magicians in the time of Moses, **Exodus 7:22:** *"Then the magicians of Egypt did so with their enchantments; and Pharaoh's heart grew hard, and he did not heed them, as the Lord had said."* **NKJV**.

The False Prophet deceived everyone with his false miracles that Satan had empowered him to do. Because of these things, the Beast made those on earth build an idol which the False Prophet caused to seem to speak, to come alive. All those followers of the Antichrist worshiped the Antichrist and were required to worship his image.

Everyone was commanded to worship the Beast, whether rich or poor, mighty or weak. All must worship and all must receive in the act of worship the mark of the Beast, 666, upon their forehead or hand. This was also a permit to buy or sell. There were no exceptions.

The Antichrist seems to be winning but the end is yet to come. God has not made His final move. It may seem as though there is no hope, but hope is about to rise and make itself known.

Never feel that because difficult times may come upon the follower of God that God is not with him. God is always present and His will, will always be done, period! Never lose faith. Always look up and keep doing what God has called you to do.

Chapter 14

Remember that the book of Revelation is not written in chronological order but in the order that John saw various things. They are noted as John sees them. We have seen the unholy trinity of Satan, the Antichrist, and the False Prophet and will soon see the false church, the church of the Antichrist, and the fall and judgment of all in the next few chapters. John now writes about several things that are included in the first half as well as the second half of the Tribulation.

Verses 1 – 5

The re-emerging of the 144,000 Prophets of God.

Now we are about to see the anticipated coming of judgment and reward. There are many things that I do not understand about God and those things are mysteries. Some things I may never know or understand, but there are many that I can come to understand.

Jesus told His disciples about the time of the end and told them that only the Father knew when it would happen, not even the angels in heaven. We cannot know the mind of God. We are not God. I wonder why God created Satan, and I do not believe that anyone can come to a clear understanding of it. Perhaps it is because He wanted to display His marvelous grace and mercy. Without a failure, a falling short of the glory of God, there would not be a need of grace and mercy. I really do not know. This is the part of faith. We just trust God because He is God and because He is good, kind, and loving. He is also just, righteous, and holy. All are measured by His holiness and with His justice and in His great wrath. I also wonder why God created gnats, mosquitoes, and flies. Perhaps it was to display His judgment upon us, but who can know? All I know is that God is my God, Jesus is my Savior, and the Holy Spirit is my Teacher, Comforter, and Guide in this life. I trust God and need not know anything more.

At this point in the Tribulation, we see that the 144,000 prophets, which had been sealed in Chapter 7, are in Jerusalem. The Temple has been rebuilt, therefore, the Muslim Dome of the Rock and Mosque have been destroyed and replaced with a new Temple in the original footprint of the Jewish Temple. Muhammad and his religion have been destroyed for there is no reference to anything close to it.

Along with Jesus, there is a great choir from heaven with many instruments who are singing of the redeemed earth. This great choir sings with the 144,000 prophets and their converts. This song of redemption is a song which the angels cannot sing or learn because they have no understanding of redemption, in that they had no need of redemption; but they like what they hear. This is a song of victory as well. These redeemed ones stand faultless before the throne of God, for His mercy and grace have been granted to them on behalf of His Son Jesus, and His righteousness has been poured over them.

What a marvelous sight and sound!

Verses 6 – 12

Following the song of the redeemed, John sees a mighty angel flying in heaven with a message and having the Good News that is to be preached to every tribe, tongue, people, and nation in the world. This is the message that was given to the church today but is also given to the 144,000 prophets. The message is the everlasting Gospel of Christ. The message is for every people, tribe, tongue, and nation on earth to fear God alone and to give Him the glory alone for He alone deserves glory. These 144,000 prophets had upon them the protection of God to proclaim the message that they had been given. They had no need to fear anyone. They served God and feared Him alone. Jesus taught His disciples that they should not fear the one who could kill the body but fear the One who could destroy both body and soul and throw them into eternal hell. **Matthew 10:28:** *"And do not fear those who kill the body but cannot kill the soul. But rather fear Him who is able to destroy both soul and body in hell."* **NKJV**.

Standing with the 144,000 are those converts who had not taken the mark of the beast. They have followed the Lamb and stand victorious with Christ Jesus. These have overcome this great time of Tribulation. **Verse 5:** *"And in their mouth was found no deceit, for they are without fault before the throne of God.* **NKJV**.

This is how and why all those who are in Christ Jesus can stand boldly before God. They confidently stand because they have upon them the righteousness of Jesus. We stand before the Throne of God faultless. **2 Corinthians 5:21:** *"For He has made Him who knew no sin to be sin for us, that we might become the righteousness of God in Him,"* **NKJV**. **Hebrews 9:27:** *"And as it is appointed for men to die once, but after this the judgment,"* **NKJV**. **2 Corinthians 5:10-11:** *"For we must all appear before the judgment seat of Christ, that each one may receive the things done in the body, according to what he has done, whether good or bad. Knowing, therefore, the terror of the Lord, we persuade men; but we are well known to God, and I also trust are well known in your consciences."* **NKJV**.

This is the same message that the 144,000 Prophets of God are proclaiming to the world. But during these seven years of Great Tribulation, the Holy Spirit is not drawing men and they must make a decision on their own power and by their own mind. So, this is what the scene will be like at the moment Christ returns.

The first angel, having proclaimed his message, is followed by a second angel who has great news for the believers of the Tribulation. The news is that the church of the Antichrist, with its lying message, has fallen and Satan has fallen as well. Great Babylon, as it is called, has been weighed in the balances of God and found to be a lie of Satan. She has caused great damage and caused many to suffer the wrath of God for following her in the worship of the Antichrist. They have the defining mark of the Antichrist worshiper upon them, the number 666.

The second angel is quickly followed by a third and final angel who has a message: **Verses 9 – 12,** " *'If anyone worships the beast and his image, and receives his mark on his forehead or on his hand, he himself shall also drink of the wine of the wrath of God, which is poured out full strength into the cup of His indignation. He shall be tormented with fire and brimstone in the presence of the holy angels and in the presence of the Lamb. And the smoke of their torment ascends forever and ever; and they have no rest day or night, who worship the beast and his image, and whoever receives the mark of his name.' Here is the patience of the saints, here are those who keep the commandments of God and the faith of Jesus."* **NKJV.**

Remember when Jesus was in the Garden of Gethsemane? He was given a cup of God's wrath to drink for the believer and He prayed three times about that bitter cup. He struggled to drink it and asked if it were possible for the Father to take the cup from Him, but He said, *"nevertheless not My will, but Yours, be done."* **Luke 22:42 NKJV.** But Jesus drank it. He drank it all, every bitter and polluted drop, for the sins of you and me. During this time, however the unrepentant must drink it all as it is poured out in full upon them.

Verse 13

The announcement comes from heaven for a blessing from God to His followers: *"Then I heard a voice from heaven saying to me, 'Write: 'Blessed are the dead who die in the Lord from now on.' 'Yes,' says the Spirit, 'that they may rest from their labors, and their works follow them.'"*

The unbelievers are tormented for eternity and the believers receive rest for eternity. Each group will receive their just judgment from God—to one, God's wrath for their unbelief and disobedience; to the other, blessing and gifts from God's good hand, a reward for their faith and obedience to God.

Verses 14 – 20

The greatly awaited proclamation announced.

The time of reaping has come. What the followers of Satan have sown has grown to maturity and now has come the harvest for their wickedness. The harvest is swift and terrible. It comes from the hand of the Son of Man, Jesus Christ, God's Only Begotten Son. They may have thought that they would go unpunished, but God's patience has come to an end.

The sharp sickle of God moves swiftly and surely. With the swing of the sickle, the clusters of the grapes of wrath are placed into the winepress of God. The grapes are fully ripened with the juice of wickedness, and they are trampled. **Verse. 20:** *"And the winepress was trampled outside the city, and blood came out of the winepress, up to the horses' bridles, for one thousand six hundred furlongs* (184 miles)." **NKJV.**

This is referring to the great Battle of Armageddon, which will soon take place. It is described in **Chapter 16** as well as in **Zachariah 14: 1-21** and **Joel 3**. I will discuss it later.

Chapter 15

Verses 1 – 8

The introduction of the Seven Bowls of Wrath from God.

John now witnesses another sign in heaven. He sees seven angels dressed in pure bright white linen and wrapped with golden bands around their chests. From the throne of God comes one of the four living creatures of God with a golden bowl for each of the seven angels. Each bowl is filled with plagues of wrath from God to be poured out in sequence upon the earth and upon the unbelievers for the rebellion that they have been unleashing against God and upon God's people.

The song of Moses and the Lamb was also sung, declaring God's great power and His righteous judgments just before the angels receive their Bowls of God's Wrath, which are great and grievous. This will be the last display of God's wrath before Jesus returns.

These seven plagues remind one of the ten plagues that God brought upon Egypt during the exodus of God's people recorded in **Exodus 7—12.** The Temple in **Chapter 15** is seen to be filled with the smoke of God's glory and power. No one was able to enter the Temple until the seven angels had completed their mission.

Chapter 16

Verse 1

The angels arrive upon earth and each prepares to pour out his bowl of wrath. As God poured His wrath upon Pharaoh and Egypt, which led to the exodus of the children of Israel from their years of slavery and their return to the land God had given them, we see God pouring out His great wrath in these final Seven Bowls of Wrath.

Verse 2

Bowl One

The wrath of God is displayed in sores, perhaps boils or ulcers, upon every person on earth that had the mark of the beast and all the worshipers of the beast or Antichrist.

Verse 3

Bowl Two

The second bowl was poured out upon the salt water of the earth, the oceans, seas, and open gulfs of salt water. They became as blood causing all the fish and all the living things that live in the seas to die. What an awful sight and sickening smell this plague created, along with the foul smell of the first bowl of wrath poured out upon the worshipers of the Antichrist.

As we read in the trumpet judgments where one third of the living things died, here all living things in the seas die (**Revelation 8:8-9**). It reminds one of the rivers being turned to blood in **Exodus 7:15-25**.

Verses 4 – 7

Bowl Three

The third bowl was poured out upon all the fresh water streams, creeks, lakes, and rivers, and they become blood. These judgments from God are terrible but just and righteous, **Verse 7**. As these followers of Satan shed the blood of the saints and the prophets, now comes the just reward of the followers of Satan, and they are given blood to drink. There is no body of fresh water left untouched. It is, as John writes in **Verse 6,** *"their just due."*

Verses 8 & 9

Bowl Four

The heat of the sun is increased upon the earth and results in blisters upon mankind. They rejected the Light of the World, the One who said, *"Let there be light,"* the One who *"came into the world to save the world,"* and the One who created the sun *"to rule the day"* which now scorches the world and man with great heat. The sun that is needed to grow and sustain life now gives pain.

The result of this judgment causes disgust from the worshipers of the Antichrist, and they blaspheme God rather than repent. The hate that they have for God comes to the top, and there is no glory within them for God at all.

Verses 10 & 11

The Fifth Bowl

The judgment of this fifth bowl is total darkness that comes upon the throne, the capital city of the Antichrist, Babylon. This is great darkness that causes tremendous fear upon the followers of the Antichrist. Not only fear, but indescribable pain comes with this darkness where people chew their tongues, and the great sores which they have cause them to express their hatred for God with great blasphemy towards Him. There is no repentance here, just hate for God.

The only solution to all this is repentance, but they reject God because their deeds are evil. This is the problem today. The only solution for sin is the forgiveness of God, and He is rejected.

Verse 12

Bowl six

The sixth bowl is poured upon the Euphrates River and it dries up, making a way for the great final battle with the Antichrist's forces of 200,000,000 from the east to move upon the city of God, Jerusalem, in the Battle of Armageddon. Here God prepares for the battle, and the troops of the east will have nothing to hinder them from the great final battle.

Verses 13 – 21

Bowl seven and the Battle of Armageddon

The result of the seventh bowl of wrath is for the final destruction of the capital city of the Antichrist. The city is called Babylon, and in **Verse 17** the angel from the Throne of God in heaven declares with a strong and victorious voice, *"It is done!"* The declaration from God's Throne is directed to the throne of the Antichrist and the message is, "It is over!"

The place of all the confusion on earth and the source of all the gross immorality, the hatred of God, the great lie, and the top liar, Satan, along with his Antichrist and False prophet, will now be targeted by God and overthrown by God. The time has come. There will be no more waiting. The One who is patient and not willing that any should perish is about to bring it all to an end. *It is done!*

At this time, we see three unclean spirits, or demons, come out of Satan, the Antichrist and the False prophet. These three evil spirits quickly do the will of Satan, and that is to bring his army from the east. They go to every country allied with Satan to gather them to come and be arrayed or prepared for battle. This is the battle of *the "great day of God Almighty,"* **Verse 14**. Paul makes mention of this day in **2 Thessalonians 1:9,** *"These shall be punished with everlasting destruction from the presence of the Lord and from the glory of His power, when He comes, in that Day, to be glorified in His saints and to be admired among all those who believe, because our testimony among you was believed."* **NKJV**

John writes in **Verse 15**, *"Behold, I am coming as a thief. Blessed is he who watches, and keeps his garments, lest he walk naked and they see his shame,"* **NKJV.** Time is quickly coming to an end and all who are not ready for His coming will suffer great and eternal loss.

One might wonder, why is it that people in those days do not see the truth and turn to God? The reason is they believe *"the lie."* Satan is The Liar and has been from the beginning. Paul writes in **2 Thessalonians 2:9-12:** *"The coming of the lawless one is according to the working of Satan, with all power, signs, and lying wonders, and with all unrighteous deception among those who perish, because they did not receive the love of the truth, that they might be saved. And for this reason God will send them strong delusion that they should believe the lie that they all may be condemned who did not believe the truth but had pleasure in unrighteousness."* **NKJV**.

Satan is a liar and a deceiver. This is what he does, and he is proficient in it. In these last times, the Holy Spirit is taken out of the way in order for the man of sin to do his works, **2 Thessalonians 2:7-8**. The Holy Spirit convicts and draws men today, and that drawing to God will not be available in the last days.

All eyes upon on the earth are focused upon this one place called *Armageddon*. The seventh angel pours out the last drop of wrath, and when he is finished, he announces with a loud voice: *"It is done!"*

Accompanying the announcement is a spontaneous and loud cheer of victory from the Throne of God in heaven. The cheer brings rumblings and lightening upon earth. Earthquakes erupt such as never witnessed before. Babylon is conquered. Satan's capital divides and falls in great and final defeat. All the great army, all 200,000,000 of them, die in the fierceness of God's great wrath. The full cup of the wrath of God is poured out upon her. It is a fearful thing to stand before the living God. John says in **Verse 20** that *"every island fled away and the mountains were not found,"* **NKJV.** The great earthquakes had sunk the islands of the earth, both small and great and caused the mountains of the earth to crumble and to be no more.

At this great battle, there were 75-pound hailstones that fell from heaven upon the forces of Satan, and they responded with even more hatred toward God because of His wrath being poured out upon them.

People are not turning to God, but rather, turning more and more away from God.

Chapter 17

Verses 1 – 6

Seven Dooms are pronounced here. The first is Babylon, "The Great Harlot Church."

God is all about worship. God created man to fellowship with Him, and to worship Him with glory, honor, and praise. That relationship was contaminated with the introduction of sin. The communion of God with man was a regular time. We read in **Genesis 3:8:** *"And they heard the sound of the Lord God walking in the garden in the cool of the day, and Adam and his wife hid themselves from the presence of the Lord God among the trees of the garden. Then the Lord God called to Adam and said to him, 'Where are you?' So, he said, 'I heard Your voice in the garden, and I was afraid because I was naked; and I hid myself.' "* **NKJV**

Sin had corrupted the Truth with a lie, and the communion between God and man changed. True worship brings man to God, and God responds favorably to our worship of Him. Now, in **Chapter 17** we have the announcement of "enough is enough," and God's strong wrath comes down hard upon this "anti-worship," that is "lying and false worship." True worship is for God alone. Here we see the worship of the Antichrist. *"Come, I will show you the judgment of the great harlot,"* **Verse 1**.

For centuries Israel and even the church had fallen to adulterous worship. Each had committed adultery in the worship of false idols and had dishonored God.

Romans 1:21-28 says, *"Because, although they knew God, they did not glorify Him as God, nor were thankful, but became* *futile in their thoughts, and their foolish hearts were darkened. Professing to be wise, they became fools, and changed the glory of the incorruptible God into an image made like corruptible man—and birds and four-footed animals and creeping things. Therefore, God also gave them up to uncleanness, in the lusts of their hearts, to dishonor their bodies among themselves, who exchanged the truth of God for the lie, and worshipped and served the creature rather than the Creator, who is blessed forever. Amen. For this reason God gave them up to vile passions. For even their women exchanged the natural use for what is against nature. Likewise also the men, leaving the natural use of the woman, burned in their lust for one another, men with men committing what is shameful, and receiving in themselves the penalty of their error which was due. And even as they did not like to retain God in their knowledge, God gave them over to a debased mind, to do those things which are not fitting;"* NKJV.

Judges 2:17 explains the religious adultery: *"Yet they would not listen to their judges, but they played the harlot with other gods, and bowed down to them. They turned quickly from the way in which their fathers walked, in obeying the commandments of the Lord; they did not do so."* **NKJV**.

God had commanded Israel not to have other gods before Him and not to worship idols, but they disobeyed and went out in unfaithfulness to God. Still, God remained faithful and here in **Revelation 17,** we read of God's pronouncement of doom to *"the great harlot"* and her worshippers of the Antichrist. God's desire is for worship, and He will get it.

The Great Harlot, *"who sits on many waters"* **NKJV**, *"over many waters"* **ESV**, *"upon many waters"* **Berean Literal Bible**, *"on raging waters,"* **God's Word Translated**, is explained in **Verse 15:** *"Then he said to me, 'The waters which you saw, where the harlot sits, are peoples, multitudes, nations, and tongues. And the ten thorns which you saw on the beast, these* *will hate the harlot, make her desolate and naked, eat her flesh and burn her with fire."* **NKJV**

The harlot has caused most of those dwellers on the earth to commit worship adultery. Her worshipers are obsessed with a great hatred of God and with a drunken, mindless, and foolish worship, allegiance to, and obsession with the Antichrist.

Paul writes in **Thessalonians 2:9-12:** *"The coming of the lawless one is according to the working of Satan, with all power, signs, and lying wonders, and with all unrighteous deception among those who perish, because they did not receive the love of the truth, that they might be saved. And for this reason God will send them <u>strong delusion</u>, that they should believe the lie, that they all may be condemned who did not believe the truth but had pleasure in unrighteousness."* **NKJV**

We see this even now. People are quick to believe "the lie" of Satan and cannot see "the Truth." They believe the delusion of Satan, and it is only through the convictive power of the Holy Spirit that mankind is drawn to the Truth; but, now the Holy Spirit has been taken out of the way to leave the Antichrist unhindered in his work. He spreads his lie and displays his delusions to those on earth unhindered by the Holy Spirit. **2 Thessalonians 2:7:** *"For the mystery of lawlessness is already at work; only He who now restrains will do so until He is taken out of the way. And then the lawless one will be revealed, whom the Lord will consume with the breath of His mouth and destroy with the brightness of His coming."* **NKJV**

In **Verses 3 – 5,** John is taken away *"in the Spirit into the wilderness."* The Spirit points out a woman in the wilderness. The woman John sees as the great harlot is dressed lavishly and adorned with every luxury and amenity that people seek on earth. They want wealth, they want power, and they want prestige. In her hand is a golden cup full of abominations to

God and the putrefying filth of her deeds and adultery. These possessions emphasize who she is: **Verse 5,** *"MYSTERY, BABYLON THE GREAT, THE MOTHER OF HARLOTS AND OF THE ABOMINATIONS OF THE EARTH."* **NKJV**

She has taken her worshipers further than they really wanted to go and caused them to do much more than they had intended to do. They are "mindless" in their deeds while she is fully purpose driven in all she planned to do. She is *"drunk with the blood of the saints and with the blood of the martyrs of Jesus,"* **Verse 6, NKJV.**

Because a believer of Christ Jesus is killed for the cause of Christ does not mean that the opposition has won. It means that the ministry that the believer has been given to do has successfully come to an end. They were victorious in what God had called them to do. It is here, in the exact center of God's timing, that judgment is enacted and victory is completed.

John says in **Verse 6** that he marveled with great amazement. John wondered, perhaps, why was this allowed? We think the same thing today as we witness gross actions against God and His people carried out by vicious followers of Satan. These evils are seemingly carried out without restriction from God. The answer is that judgment has not yet come; but judgment will come, and it will be unhindered, sure, and eternal. It will not come until the appointed time in God's timing.

Verses 7 – 18

John marvels at what he sees, and the angel explains to him what he is seeing. This "great harlot" is the Satan empowered church of the Antichrist. With the great harlot, Babylon is a union of ten kings from ten countries who have joined with the Babylon church. Her doom is already pronounced to be sure and eternal. All will marvel at her, adore her, and join in worship with her. Only those who have their names written in The Lamb's Book of Life will see her as who she is and what she is.

The location of the great harlot is Babylon. The city sits upon seven mountains or hills, which are the seven heads that John sees. Many scholars believe this to be Rome, which is often described as "the city on seven hills." The sure identity of this city and its location is uncertain. It can only be a guess. The certainty here is that it will be a real city, at an exact location, and it will sit gloriously built as an impressive city and center or capital of the Antichrist and his church.

The seven kings, five of whom have already come and one which is present at the writing of Revelation, are Egypt, Assyria, Babylon, Medo-Persia, Greece, and Rome. Rome was the present kingdom, the *"one that is."* The seventh is the kingdom of the Antichrist. John writes in **Verse 11,** *"The beast that was, and is not, is himself also the eighth, and is of the seven, and is going to perdition."* **NKJV**. This verse is a difficult one to have sure understanding. Perhaps the *'beast that was, and is not, is himself also the eighth, and is of the seven"* is about being killed and brought back to life at the resurrection of the three witnesses in **Revelation 13:3 & 12-13**. This eighth "kingdom of the beast" is perhaps a continuation of the seventh kingdom of Rome. This is mere speculation.

In **Verses 12 & 13**, we read that this alliance of ten kingdoms, which have not come into being at the writing of Revelation, will have profound influence with world governments and will be an aid to the Antichrist. This will be a brief giving the power that they must to the Antichrist, Verse **13**.

This evil alliance will make war with the Lamb, but the Lamb will devour them for He is King of Kings and Lord of Lords. This battle or event is about to take place.

The waters are *"peoples, multitudes, nations, and tongues"* of the world, **Verse 15.** Though this is an alliance, they will turn on the church of the Antichrist and devour her and burn her, **Verses 16 & 17**. Why? It is because God will use them as a tool of His judgment. *"For God has put it into their hearts to fulfill His purpose, to be of one mind, and to give their kingdom to the beast, until the words of God are fulfilled,"* **Revelation 17:17 NKJV**. In **Romans 13:1:** *"Let every soul be subject to the governing authorities. For there is no authority except from God, and the authorities that exist are appointed by God,"* **NKJV**. **Matthew 28:18** says, *"And Jesus came and spoke to them, saying, 'All authority has been given to Me in heaven and on earth,' "* **NKJV**. The bottom line is that God is always in control and uses all things for His glory. He is Sovereign over all.

So, the Great harlot is destroyed. Her doom is announced.

Chapter 18

Verses 1 – 24

The second doom, Babylon

The announcement of the **second doom or verdict** now comes: *"'Babylon the great is fallen, is fallen, and has become a dwelling place of demons, a prison for every foul spirit, and a cage for every unclean and hated bird!' "* **Verse 2.** The city that was so elegant has become the hideout of demons, nest of vultures, and home of the despised animals of the earth.

Babylon has often been related to opposition to God and used by God as well as a punishment upon His chosen people, Israel, for its religious unfaithfulness. Babylon is now used by Satan and is the headquarters or capital city of the Antichrist.

The entire world has been contaminated by its great sin and has benefited in the relationship that the various nations have had through trade. Great wealth has come to the nations because of their bowing down to Satan. As Satan tempted Jesus in **Matthew 4:1-11** with power, prestige, and glory, he fulfilled the desires of the nations with those very things. But this was about to end.

Verse 3: *"For all the nations have drunk of the wine of the wrath of her fornication, the kings of the earth have committed fornication with her, and the merchants of the earth have become rich through the abundance of her luxury."* **NKJV.**

There is also a warning that came with this verdict of doom, and it was given to the followers of Christ Jesus, those converts of the 144,000 prophets of God. The warning was for those believers who were there to come out, or to get out of the city, so they would not be affected by her plagues. This warning reminds one of the warning that the angels gave to Lot just before God destroyed Sodom and Gomorrah in **Genesis 19:12-29**. Doom and destruction were eminent and escape was still possible for those who would obey God's warning. God would now unleash His wrath for her great iniquities.

As the announcement of her doom comes, which will come quickly, it will be all consuming and great in wrath. She will be *"utterly burned."* **Hebrews 10:31 NKJV** says, *"It is a fearful thing to fall into the hands of the living God,"* and that is where Babylon finds herself, *"for strong is the Lord God who judges her,"* **Verse 8, NKJV**.

At her destruction, there is great mourning by the world system, the followers of Babylon, because they had benefited by her greatly. This mourning is a selfish one, *"for no one buys their merchandise anymore: merchandise of gold and silver, precious stones and pearls, fine linen and purple, silk and scarlet, every kind of citron wood, every kind of object of ivory, every kind of object of most precious wood, bronze, iron, and marble; and cinnamon and incense, fragrant oil and frankincense, wine and oil, fine flour and wheat, cattle and sheep, horses and chariots, and bodies and souls of men. The fruit that your soul longed for has gone from you, and all the things which are rich and splendid have gone from you, and you shall find them no more at all. The merchants of these things, who became rich by her, will stand at a distance for fear of her torment, weeping and wailing, and saying, 'Alas, alas, that great city that was clothed in fine linen, purple and scarlet, and adorned with gold and precious stones and pearls! For in one hour such great riches came to nothing.' "Verses* **11-17, NKJV**

Yes, this weeping by the world system was all about self. They were as pitiful and shameful as was Babylon and the Great Harlot. Did you notice the slave trade and human trafficking that was associated with the Harlot, Babylon, and her beneficiaries as referred to in **Verse 13,** *"and bodies and souls of men,"* **NKJV**? Satan enslaves all his followers and his followers enslave others as well: *"for by your sorcery all the nations were deceived,"* **Verse 23, NKJV**. Satan is a liar, a deceiver, and a killer of the saints and prophets on the earth.

Chapter 19

Verses 1 – 10

The rejoicing in heaven.

Those in heaven rejoice in the doom of Babylon and the Great Harlot. What has just been witnessed is the mighty hand of God's great and awesome judgment being carried out. Salvation, glory, honor, power, and praise belong to God and Him alone.

God's judgments are true and right. The judgment of God is not a one-time thing and it's over. God's judgment is an eternal one that will last for eternity. Every person on earth has a choice as far as eternity is concerned: eternal life or eternal death.

Praise rises loud and strong in heaven because everyone realizes that God's eternal reign has begun and that the church, the bride of Christ, has made herself ready. The marriage of the Lamb, Jesus Christ, to His bride the church, is announced.

John describes the bride of Christ. He finds the bride of Christ arrayed in pure, fine and brilliant linen. That fine linen of her gown is the righteous acts of the saints done on earth, **Verse 8**. The party is about to begin and the great rejoicing will follow.

There is a wedding announcement and it reads: *"Blessed are those who are called to the marriage supper of the Lamb!"* **Verse 9**. John is asked to write this announcement, and the glory of writing it causes John to fall at the feet of the angel, who quickly cautions him to rise because only God is worthy of worship. Worship is what God is all about, and worshipping

God is what the believer is all about. *"Worship God!"* **Verse 10, NKJV.**

Verses 11 – 16

The appearance of Jesus on the white horse.

John says, *"Now I saw heaven opened, and behold, a white horse. And He who sat on him was called Faithful and True, and in righteousness, He judges and makes war,"* **Revelation 19:11 NKJV.** There is a significant difference in the one described on the white horse here in **Revelation 19:11** and the one in **Revelation 6:2:** *"And I looked, and behold, a white horse. He who sat on it had a bow; and a crown given to him, and he went out conquering and to conquer,"* **NKJV.**

Both riders are sitting on a white horse but that is where the similarity ends. The horse is not the significant thing but rather the one sitting on the horse is. In **Chapter 6:2,** the rider had *"a bow and a crown given to him."* The bow was given to him as was the crown, but they were allowed for him to have for a predetermined time. The bow was to be used in his quest in conquering and to conquer. This rider was a rebel with the desire to overcome and to be like the King of Kings and His followers, and his weapon was a bow to wound and kill. The rider on the horse in **Chapter 19:11** is known for His Faithfulness and Truth and is called by that earned name. This rider is the Truth, the Way, and the Life. The rider is the only way to the Father (**John 14:6**).

The rider in **Chapter 6:2,** being a rebel, is also a dissenter and an accuser of the brethren, **Revelation 12:10:** *"Then I heard a loud voice saying in heaven, 'Now salvation, and strength, and the kingdom of our God, and the power of His Christ have come, for the accuser of our brethren, who accused them before our God day and night, has been cast down.' "* **NKJV**

The rider in **Chapter 19:11** had many crowns, **verse 12**. The rider is already King of Kings, and He does not need to conquer, for He already possesses the universe and everything therein. Every knee will bow before Him, **Philippians 2:9-11:** *"Therefore God also has highly exalted Him and given Him the name which is above every name, that at the name of Jesus every knee should bow, of those in heaven, and of those on earth, and of those under the earth, and that every tongue should confess that Jesus Christ is Lord, to the glory of God the Father."* **NKJV**

Jesus, being judge, will pronounce judgment upon the rider in **Chapter 6:2** as well. The rider in **Chapter 19:11** comes to judge all and He overcomes all by the sword of His word or by His decree. **Chapter 19:21:** *"And the rest were killed with the sword which proceeded from the mouth of Him who sat on the horse. And all the birds were filled with their flesh."* **NKJV**

The rider in **Chapter 6:2** is the Antichrist and the rider in **Chapter 19:11** is The Christ. The appearance of Jesus Christ brings doom to all those on the battlefield of Armageddon, to the Antichrist, and to the False Prophet, **Verse 20:** *"Then the beast was captured, and with him the false prophet who worked signs in his presence, by which he deceived those who received the mark of the beast and those who worshipped his image. These two were cast alive into the lake of fire burning with brimstone."* **NKJV**

The rider of the white horse in **Chapter 19:11** is described further:

- His eyes were like flames of fire, **Verse 12**
- On His head were many crowns, **Verse 12**
- He had a secret name, **Verse 12**
- He wore a blood dripped robe, **Verse 13**
- He is called The Word of God, **Verse 13**

- His warrior angels and followers ride behind Him on white horses but they do not do the fighting. The fight is the Lord's and His weapon of mass destruction is His word, **Verses 14-15**
- He is awesome in power, **Verse 15**
- His name is written on His robe and on His thigh: King of Kings and Lord of Lords, **Verse 16**

We see that Jesus comes with intense wrath to inflict great vengeance. He has the authority to do what He comes to do, for He is King of Kings and Lord of Lords, which is the secret name, perhaps an endearing name, given Him by the Father, and is known only by the Father and Holy Spirit. It is for sure a beloved one for He is the Only Begotten Son of God. **John 3:16:** *"For God so loved the world that He gave His only begotten Son. . ."* **NKJV**. *"Therefore God also has highly exalted Him and given Him the name which is above every name, that at the name of Jesus every knee should bow, of those in heaven, and of those on earth, and of those under the earth, and that every tongue should confess that Jesus Christ is Lord, to the glory of God the Father."* **Philippians 2:9-11 NKJV**

We also see a blood dripped robe which He wears. This robe is soaked with the blood of Jesus which He freely shed. Though His sacrifice, an act of great Godly love, was more than sufficient to wash away all the sin of all mankind, it is applied only to those who would believe in Him and receive His free gift of salvation. Those who reject His gift remain condemned in their sin. What an awful thought that some would reject so great a gift! *"For God did not send His Son into the world to condemn the world, but that the world through Him might be saved. He who believes in Him is not condemned; but he who does not believe is condemned already, because he has not believed in the name of the only begotten Son of God."* **John 3:17-18 NKJV**

The Second Coming of Christ.

Jesus now comes and places His feet upon the Mount of Olives to take care of business and to set up His Millennial Kingdom on earth. This is not the Rapture. At the Rapture, the saints were caught up to meet the Lord in the air. The raptured saints are now returning with Christ to rule with Him for a thousand years in His new kingdom.

At the Ascension of Christ, the angels informed those who witnessed it. As they stood there, awe-struck and amazed, an angel gave them information as to Christ's return.

Acts 1:6 – 11 *"Therefore, when they had come together, they asked Him, saying, 'Lord, will You at this time restore the kingdom to Israel?' And He said to them, 'It is not for you to know times or seasons which the Father has put in His own authority. But you shall receive power when the Holy Spirit has come upon you; and you shall be witnesses to Me in Jerusalem, and in all Judea and Samaria, and to the end of the earth.' Now when He had spoken these things, while they watched, He was taken up, and a cloud received Him out of their sight. And while they looked steadfastly toward heaven as He went up, behold, two men stood by them in white apparel, who also said, 'Men of Galilee, why do you stand gazing up into heaven? This same Jesus, who was taken up from you into heaven, will so come in like manner as you saw Him go into heaven.' "* **NKJV**

Jesus came the first time to save, and now He comes to bring judgment and wrath. Why would anyone not choose life, but freely and purposefully chose death? *"See, I have set before you today life and good, death and evil, in that I command you today to love the Lord your God, to walk in His ways. . . therefore choose life, that both you and your descendants may live;"* **Deuteronomy 30:15-19 NKJV**.

The blood of Jesus is sufficient for the sin of all. His sacrifice was a one-time act and nothing else remains to be done other than to admit your sin and confess Him as Savior, Lord, and soon coming King. **Hebrews 9:27:** *"And as it is appointed for men to die once, but after this the judgment, so Christ was offered once to bear the sins of many. To those who eagerly wait for Him He will appear a second time, apart from sin, for salvation,"* **NKJV**. *"But this Man, after He had offered one sacrifice for sins forever, sat down at the right hand of God, from that time waiting till His enemies are made His footstool. For by one offering He has perfected forever those who are being sanctified."* **Hebrews 10:12–14 NKJV**.

The rider here on the white horse is called "The Word of God." We read in John's gospel as he describes Jesus with the same name. He begins his gospel with these words: *"In the beginning was the Word, and the Word was with God, and the Word was God,"* **John 1:1 NKJV**. Jesus is The Word. The rider now comes to bring judgment and enact the wrath of God to the unbelievers, Satan, and all that is evil.

In preparation for Jesus' swift and awesome display of God's wrath, an angel standing in the brightness of the sun, makes a loud and fearful announcement. The call of this mighty angel is to the vultures to come for a great feast. The feast will be the flesh of those on the battlefield of Armageddon. All will die, both the small and the insignificant of earth as well as the great ones of the earth. Those who are free along with those who are slaves will die. Captains, mighty men of valor along with their kings and the horses upon which they sit, all those who had the mark of the beast, and all those who worshipped his image will all die together. Swift and sure is the judgment. Satan, the Antichrist, and the False Prophet will be captured and thrown into the lake of fire.

It is truly a fearful thing to stand before the living God (**Hebrews 10:31**). And great and swift was the fall! The conclusion is **Verse 21:** *"And the rest were killed with the sword which proceeded from the mouth of Him who sat on the horse. And all the birds were filled with their flesh."* **NKJV**

Chapter 20

Verses 1 – 3

Four dooms or verdicts have been announced so far:

1. The Great Harlot, **Revelation 17:1-18**
2. Babylon, **Revelation 18:1-24**
3. Armageddon, **Revelation 19:17-21**
4. The Antichrist and False Prophet, **Revelation 19:19**

We will now witness the remaining three dooms to be announced:

5. God and Magog, **Revelation 20:7-10**
6. Satan, **Revelation 20:1 – 3 & 10**
7. The unsaved at the Great White Throne Judgment, **Revelation 20:11-15**

We read in **Revelation 20:1** of another mighty angel who swiftly comes down from heaven. He has in his possession the key to the bottomless pit and a great chain in his hand. He comes to fulfill a directive from God.

This angel is commanded by God to take hold of Satan and chain him. I guess I could say that this angel is doing the "light work" of God. The personal hand of God is not needed for this mission to conquer Satan. It is not necessary for God Himself to do anything other than send another angel to confine Satan. After all, Satan is also an angel.

To the believer, this says that if God has called us to do something which is His will for us, then we are invincible in performing that call, that mission of God's will. We do not do anything in our own power but through and by the power of God. Never doubt the success of something God has called you to do. All we must do is to obey and God provides all the rest. Just do your best and leave God the rest.

This angel takes hold of Satan, or arrests him, not by his own power but at the command and by the authority and power of God. He chains Satan, disables him, and opens the bottomless pit with the key that God has given him. The angel places God's seal upon Satan and then casts him into the bottomless pit.

This humiliates Satan for it is the first time Satan has ever been "angel handled," I could say, in the same way we might say of someone being overcome by another person as being "man handled." Now Michael the archangel did fight over the body of Moses. We read of this in **Jude 9**: *"Yet Michael the archangel, in contending with the devil, when he disputed about the body of Moses, dared not bring against him a reviling accusation, but said, 'The Lord rebuke you!' "* **NKJV**.

We do read of two archangels:

- Michael the archangel, relating to the nation of Israel
- Gabriel, who brings announcements, directives, and commands from God to specific individuals, and who enforces the will of God at God's command.

Daniel 8:16: *"And I heard a man's voice between the banks of the Ulai, who called, and said, Gabriel, make this man understand the vision."* **NKJV**

Daniel 9:21: *"Yes, while I was speaking in prayer, the man Gabriel, whom I had seen in the vision at the beginning, being caused to fly swiftly, reached me about the time of the evening offering."* **NKJV**

Daniel 10:13: *"But the prince of the kingdom of Persia withstood me twenty-one days; and behold, Michael, one of the* *chief princes, came to help me, for I had been left alone there with the kings of Persia."* **NKJV**

Luke 1:26: *"Now in the sixth month the angel <u>Gabriel</u> was sent by God to a city of Galilee named Nazareth, to a virgin betrothed to a man whose name was Joseph, of the house of David. The virgin's name was Mary."* **NKJV**

These are a few references where we read in Scripture of the archangels of God. Satan, too, was *"... the anointed cherub who covers; I established you; You were on the holy mountain of God; You walked back and forth in the midst of fiery stones. You were perfect in your ways from the day you were created, till iniquity was found in you."* **Ezekiel 28:14-15 NKJV**

This former "angel of prominence" is now captured, chained, and imprisoned in the bottomless pit. His evil work is completely stopped for one thousand years. After this designated time, he will be released for a season.

"And he cast him into the bottomless pit, and shut him up, and set a seal on him, so that he should deceive the nations no more till the thousand years were finished. But after these things he must be released for a little while." **Revelation 20:3 NKJV**

Notice the following:

- Satan is captured at the command of God. **Verses 1-2:** *"an angel coming down from heaven,"*
- Satan is restrained by the command of God. **Verse 2:** *"He laid hold of the dragon, that serpent of old, who is the Devil and Satan,"*
- Satan is disarmed by God's angel. **Verse 2:** *"and bound him for a thousand years;*
- Satan is imprisoned at the command of God. **Verse 3:** *"and he cast him into the bottomless pit, and shut him up,"*

- Satan is sealed up and God placed His seal of authority on Satan. **Verse 3**
- Satan has God's seal on him, which means that Satan could do nothing without God's approval. **Verse 3**
- Satan's work of deception and discord would come to an end for one thousand years. **Verse 3**
- Satan would have a last fling at the conclusion of this one thousand years, but it would only be for a brief time. **Verse 3**

Verses 4 – 6

The Thousand-Year Reign of Christ, or the Millennial Reign of Christ

John writes of the Millennial Reign:

"And I saw thrones, and they sat on them, and judgment was committed to them. Then I saw the souls of those who had been beheaded for their witness to Jesus and for the word of God, who had not worshiped the beast or his image, and had not received his mark on their foreheads or on their hands. And they lived and reigned with Christ Jesus for a thousand years." **Revelation 20:4 NKJV**

Paul writes of the Millennial Reign:

- **1 Corinthians 6:2:** *Do you not know that the saints will judge the world? And if the world will be judged by you, are you unworthy to judge the smallest matters?* **NKJV**

- Paul also writes of the Rapture of the Saints before the Tribulation:
  1 Thessalonians 4:16-17: *"For the Lord Himself will descend from heaven with a shout, with the voice of an archangel, and with the trumpet of God. And the dead in Christ will rise first. Then we who are alive and*

remain shall be caught up together with them in the clouds to meet the Lord in the air. And thus we shall always be with the Lord." **NKJV**

There is something interesting here to note. When the believers are taken up or raptured up in clouds, at that very moment there is not one believer, saint of God, or follower of Jesus who is left on the earth. The graves have opened and the believers have been resurrected to meet the Lord in the air. After this happens, in the twinkling of an eye, **all** the living believers are taken up or raptured to be with the Lord forever. There remains no believer left on earth. The Holy Spirit removes Himself for those seven years of tribulation to leave Satan unrestrained in his evil works. Therefore, it becomes very difficult for mankind to become a follower of Christ Jesus. The Holy Spirit, who <u>convicts</u> men of sin, is removed and all of mankind now must be <u>convinced</u> of their sin and their need of God by the preaching of the 144,000 prophets.

Jesus says of those days of tribulation in **Matthew 24:22:** *"And unless those days were shortened, no flesh would be saved; but for the elect's sake those days will be shortened."* **NKJV**

Paul tells Timothy in **2 Timothy 3:1:** *"But know this, that in the last days perilous times will come:"* **NKJV**.

Very soon after this taking up, or Rapture, God calls 144,000 new believers, which are all sealed Jewish prophets of God, who will then be God's representatives and prophets throughout the seven years of God's Great Tribulation.

At the Return of Christ, the Second Coming, and the setting up of His Earthly Kingdom for 1,000 years, which is called the Millennial Reign of Christ, there will not be a single unbeliever alive. Satan will be cast into the bottomless pit to remain there for 1,000 years.

Take a moment for a comparison of the <u>Rapture</u> of the Saints to meet and be with Christ and the <u>Second Coming</u> of Christ with the Saints.

- At the Rapture, the dead in Christ are resurrected to meet the Lord in the air. This is the <u>beginning of the first resurrection</u>. **1 Thessalonians 4:16:** *"For the Lord Himself will descend from heaven with a shout, with the voice of an archangel, and with the trumpet of God. And the dead in Christ will rise first. Then we who are alive and remain shall be caught up together with them in the clouds to meet the Lord in the air. And thus we shall always be with the Lord."* **NKJV.**

- At the Second Coming, those who have died and have not received the mark of the beast are resurrected. This is the conclusion of the <u>first resurrection</u>. **Revelation 20:4:** *"And I saw thrones, and they sat on them and judgment was committed to them. Then I saw the souls of those who had been beheaded for their witness to Jesus and for the word of God, who had not worshiped the beast or his image, and had not received his mark on their foreheads or on their hands. And they lived and reigned with Christ for a thousand years. But the rest of the dead did not live again until the thousand years were finished. This is the first resurrection. Blessed and holy is he who has part in the first resurrection. Over such the second death has no power, but they shall be priests of God and of Christ, and shall reign with Him a thousand years."* **NKJV.**

- At the Rapture, those who are alive and remain are caught up together with the resurrected to meet the Lord in clouds. **1 Thessalonians 4:17**.

- At the Second Coming, those who came out of the Tribulation, the 144,000 prophets and their converts, will enter Christ's Kingdom. **Revelation 14:1:** *"Then I looked, and behold, a Lamb standing on Mount Zion,* *and with Him one hundred and forty-four thousand, having His Father's name written on their foreheads."* **NKJV**.

- At the Rapture, the Holy Spirit is "taken out of the way" from the earth to leave Satan unrestrained. **2 Thessalonians 2:7:** *"For the mystery of lawlessness is already at work; only He who now restrains will do so until He is taken out of the way."* **NKJV**.
- At the Second Coming, Satan is imprisoned or taken out of the way for 1,000 years for the sake of Christ's Kingdom on earth. It will be a time of rest for those coming out of the Tribulation and the billions who will have been born during those 1,000 years. They will not experience the pull of sin, for the Liar and Deceiver is nowhere to be found. The earth will be sin free for 1,000 years.
- During this First Resurrection. The believers, those individuals whose names are written in the Lamb's Book of Life, will be judged for the works that they have done on earth. Paul writes of this "Judgment Seat of Christ" or the "Bema" in **2 Corinthians 5:10-11,** *"For we must all appear before the judgment seat of Christ, that each one may receive the things done in the body, according to what he has done, whether good or bad. Knowing, therefore, the terror of the Lord we persuade men; but we are well known to God, and I also trust are well known in your consciences,"* **NKJV**, and also in **Romans 14:10-13,** *"But why do you judge your brother? Or why do you show contempt for your brother? For we shall all stand before the judgment seat of Christ. For it is written: 'As I live, says the Lord, every knee shall bow to Me, and every tongue shall confess to God.' So each of us shall give account of himself to God. Therefore let us not judge one another anymore, but rather resolve this, not to put a stumbling block or a cause to fall in our brother's way,"* **NKJV**. Those names

that are written in the Lamb's Book of Life are given rewards, or crowns that they have won, and will have the glory of laying them down at the feet of Christ. Those believers who have been found unworthy of the reward or crown will have that reward or crown taken away from them, which will be to their shame.

Verses 7 – 10

The thousand-year imprisonment of Satan comes to anend.

Verse 7: *"Now when the thousand years have expired, Satan will be released from his prison and will go out to deceive the nations which are in the four corners of the earth, Gog and Magog, to gather them together to battle, whose number is as the sand of the sea."* **NKJV.**

What is happening here? Well, what is happening is that billions of people have been born in this sin-free Kingdom. They have not had any reason to feel the pull of sin for the one who is sin has been imprisoned. These children of the Kingdom of Christ have never experienced sin at all. Those who were born in this Kingdom of Christ and after the Tribulation have no idea of the great wrath of God, for there has not been a reason in all their life to witness it. All they know is what they have been taught by their family, Christ Jesus, and the Saints.

John writes that Satan's release is to *"deceive the nations."* The great deception is the Lie of Satan. A lie is anything less than the truth. It is something that falls short of the truth. To fall short of the truth is to lie. **Romans 3:23** states: *"For all have sinned and fall short of the glory of God."* **NKJV.**

Those born during the sin-free, disease-free, death-free time of these past 1,000 years have not had the chance to choose Christ. Now they are given the chance to choose. Billions of people make the wrong choice, *"whose number is as the sands of the sea,"* **Verse 8, NKJV.** These people are from all corners of the earth. They are from all nations of the earth. Their leader is Gog and Magog.

Gog and Magog might perhaps be said this way: King Gog from Magog. The nations and the billions of followers of this Satan-empowered King, Gog and Magog and their followers, are those of the **Fifth Doom**.

These are destroyed in the blink of an eye. They come and surround Jerusalem, **Verse 9:** *"They went up on the breadth of the earth and surrounded the camp of the saints and the beloved city. And fire came down from God out of heaven and devoured them. The devil, who deceived them, was cast into the lake of fire and brimstone where the beast and the false prophet are. And they will be tormented day and night forever and ever."* **NKJV.**

Satan, too, is cast into the lake of fire and brimstone. This is the **Sixth Doom,** which is the doom of Satan. The torment of hell is forever and ever. It is unending. Satan is No More!

Verses 11 – 15

The judgment of the Wicked. The Seventh and Last Doom.

The Great White Throne Judgment is witnessed.

"Then I saw a great white throne and Him who sat on it, from whose face the earth and the heaven fled away. And there was found no place for them. And I saw the dead, small and great, standing before God, and books were opened.

And another book was opened, which is the Look of Life. And the dead were judged according to their works, by the things which were written in the books. The sea gave up the dead who were in it, and Death and Hades delivered up the dead who were in them. And they were judged, each one according to his works. Then Death and Hades were cast into the lake of fire. This is the second death. And anyone not found written in the Book of Life was cast into the lake of fire." **Verses 11 – 15, NKJV**

I hear people say over and over, "I want justice, let justice be done." Justice is not what is needed here. What is needed here is mercy and grace. Jesus gives us mercy and grace.

Grace: Getting what one does not deserve. What all mankind does not deserve is heaven. The reward of heaven is made available because of grace. Justice demands hell. Grace says, "No." **Mercy:** Not getting what one deserves. What we deserve is justice, and justice would mean hell. Mercy does not give what justice demands. Justice demands hell. Mercy says, "No."

Grace and mercy are not considered at the Great White Throne Judgment. What is considered at the Great White Throne Judgment is justice for what one has done. All who are there are judged by what they have done, both the good and the bad. Everyone is judged by their deeds, but their deeds are evil. It only takes one bad or evil deed to sentence one to eternal Hell.

There are many books at the Great White Throne Judgement. There is nothing that has been done, thought or intended to do, that has not been recorded accurately in these books. God knows not only what a person has done but He knows every thought and intent of the heart, **Jeremiah 17:9-10:** *"The heart is deceitful above all things,* *and desperately wicked; who can know it? I, the Lord, search the heart, I test the mind, even to give every man according to his ways, according to the fruit of his doings,"* **NKJV**. Every person there has a book with his or her deeds written in it. The only book where their name is not found is the one that matters, The Lamb's Book of Life. Our books are the books of death.

There is great fear here, and there is no place to hide. The all-seeing, ever-present, all-powerful, and all-knowing eye of God is focused upon all, and He has not changed His mind. Yes, it is a fearful thing to stand in the presence of the living God, **Hebrews 10:31**.

Found here at the Great White Throne Judgement are the important and significant people of the earth, as well as those considered to be unimportant and insignificant. There can be found the great and mighty ones, as well as the weak and helpless ones. As one surveys the judgment hall, there is a discovery of both slaves and free-born people. The wealthy are there with the poor. Easily found are great multitudes of those who had even been pastors of churches. There are those that humanity might call "good people."

Jesus tells of this time in **Matthew 7:21-23:** *"Not everyone who says to Me, 'Lord, Lord,' shall enter the kingdom of heaven, but he who does the will of My Father in heaven. Many will say to Me in that day, 'Lord, Lord, have we not prophesied in Your name, cast out demons in Your name, and done many wonders in Your name?' And then I will declare to them, 'I never knew you; depart from Me, you who practice lawlessness,"* **NKJV**. That ought to be a wake-up call to many. He who has an ear let him hear.

Did you know Jesus didn't come to make people good? He came to give life to the spiritually dead. Being good is not the mark. Having one's name written in the Lamb's Book of Life is what it is all about.

Evil is rejecting the free gift that God's only begotten Son, Jesus, came to give, **John 3:17-18**. Evil is refusing to see the importance of having one's name written in the Lamb's Book of Life. Evil is feeling that one is good enough to go to heaven on his own merit or his own good works.

Death has presented all its dead. The sea has given up all who have died within it. Hell surrenders those within it. It is Jesus who conquered sin, death, and the grave, **1 Corinthians 15:54-57**: *"So when this corruptible has put on incorruption, and this mortal has put on immortality, then shall be brought to pass the saying that is written: 'Death is swallowed up in victory. O Death, where is your sting? O Hades, where is your victory?' The sting of death is sin, and the strength of sin is the law. But thanks be to God, who gives us the victory through our Lord Jesus Christ."* **NKJV**

Here is the good news: Death and Hades are cast into the lake of fire. This is the second death. The second death will not touch those who are part of the first resurrection. There are no believers at the Great White Throne Judgment for their names are written in the Lamb's Book of Life.

God does not have to look in the Lamb's Book of Life to search for your name, because He knows His sheep and they know His voice. The Lamb's Book of Life is a document of evidence of their guilt for all those who are lost. Therefore, Jesus says to them, "Depart from Me. I never knew you. Depart into everlasting fire and judgment." **Matthew 25:41-46; Matthew 7:21-23; John 10:13-14 & 25-30**.

"And anyone not found written in the Book of Life was cast into the lake of fire." **Verse 15, NKJV**.

This is my question to you, dear reader: Is your name written in the Lamb's Book of Life? If not, there is another book, and it has your name on it. It contains all the things you have done and will do. Make the conscious choice of Christ Jesus. Take the grace and mercy that He offers to you. You don't need to get your life together before you act. You will never be able to do that. Jesus is the only one who can do that for you. He wants you just as you are so that He can make you into what you cannot be on your own, a New Creation in Christ Jesus. Take His righteousness, and He will take your sin on Himself.

2 Corinthians 5:21: *"For He made Him who knew no sin to be sin for us, that we might become the righteousness of God in Him."* **NKJV**

2 Corinthians 5:17: *"Therefore, if anyone is in Christ, he is a new creation; old things have passed away; behold, all things have become new."* **NKJV**

Chapter 21

Verses 1 – 8

God's Wonders in the New Heaven, the New Earth and the New Jerusalem revealed

The first thing to come into view after the conclusion of the Great White Throne Judgment is new. John sees "all the new things." We read in **Verse 5:** *"Then He who sat on the throne said, 'Behold, I make all things new.' And He said to me, 'Write, for these words are true and faithful."* **NKJV**.

All things have now been made new. They are new creations. These things are not reproductions, but they are new and improved. In the first chapter of **Genesis** at the creation of the heavens and the earth, after each new day of creation God looked at what was done and He said that *"it was good."* How can one improve on good? There is good, better, and best. What God has done here is that He has removed the element that made the good bad. All things are made new without the touch or memory of Satan. He is gone and all things are new.

John is told that what he has heard, *"Behold I make all things new,"* is both a true statement and a faithful one, **Verse 5**. What was created good had been contaminated by an outside element, Satan. Now, all things are created sinless, without the evil touch of Satan.

Sin had corrupted the earth and the universe when Satan was cast out of heaven to the earth. He was cast out of heaven when sin was found in Him. As Satan was excommunicated from heaven, he took with him one-third of all the created angels. **Revelation 12:9:** *"So the great* *dragon was cast out, that serpent of old, called the Devil and Satan, who deceives the whole world; he was cast to the earth, and his angels were cast out with him,"* **NKJV**. **Revelation 12:4; Isaiah 14:12-15; Ezekiel 28:11-19**.

Therefore, God is extinguishing all memory of Satan and erasing every place where his feet may have touched. God is making *"all things new."*

What do these new created things look like? John writes to describe in words what no eye has ever seen. He can only use familiar words in his quest to describe that which has never been seen before. The reader can only imagine what he sees. **Ephesians 3:20:** *"Now to Him who is able to do exceedingly abundantly above all that we ask or think, according to the power that works in us."* **NKJV**. **1 Corinthians 2:16** *"For 'who has known the mind of the Lord that he may instruct Him?' But we have the mind of Christ."* **NKJV**

Now John begins his task. He sees a new heaven, because Satan was in the old heaven. This heaven has not been touched with the presence of Satan. John sees a new earth as well. The old earth and all that was in it was ravaged by the evil influence of Satan. The old earth was sin infested and nothing remained as it was when God created it. So, God has created a new earth for His people to enjoy, a new Eden.

The reason for the new earth is that the first earth had passed away or had been destroyed. Peter writes of this in **2 Peter 3: 10-13**, **"***But the day of the Lord will come as a thief in the night, in which the heavens will pass away with a great noise, and the elements will melt with fervent heat; both the earth and the works that are in it will be burned up. Therefore, since all these things will be dissolved, what manner of persons ought you to be in holy conduct, and* *godliness, looking for and hastening the coming of the day of God, because of which the heavens will be dissolved, being on fire, and the elements will melt with fervent heat? Nevertheless we, according to His promise, look for new heavens and a new earth in which righteousness dwells."* **NKJV**

May I pause here to say that this total destruction will not come by some tool or invention of mankind. There is no bomb or invention of man that could do what God is going to do. The tool of God's mass destruction is His Word. God is the Creator and only the Creator can wipe out that which He has created. Man, in his greatest display of wrath, may try but his most awesome invention pales to the wrath of God. *"It is a fearful thing to fall into the hands of the living God."* **Hebrews 10:31 NKJV**.

So, God in His wrath has destroyed all that was, and in His great love begins anew.

We also read in **Verse 1** that there is no more sea. Most likely this is referring to a separation of God's personal and visible presence which is now in heaven but then will be upon the new earth. We shall see Him as He is then. God will dwell with man in that new city of worship, the New Jerusalem. **Verses 2-3:** *"Then I, John, saw the holy city, New Jerusalem, coming down out of heaven from God, prepared as a bride adorned for her husband. And I heard a loud voice from heaven saying, 'Behold, the tabernacle of God is with men, and He will dwell with them, and they shall be His people. God Himself will be with them and be their God."* **NKJV**.

There is no separation of God and man in heaven. God's presence is visually witnessed and personally felt by all. They are His people and He is their God. What a comforting statement!

The New Jerusalem is seen coming down out of the new heaven and this new place of worship is adorned as a bride is adorned at her wedding. It is a beautiful thing to see a lovely bride walking the aisle to meet her new husband. Those in attendance stand in honor of the bride and stand there in awe as well. This is how John sees the New Jerusalem making her appearance on the newly created Earth.

Now there is no cause for tears for eternity. Now there is no fear of death, for there is no death. Death has lost its sting. Now there is nothing to cause worry and nothing to bring tears of loss, nor is there any pain, for all things are new, *"for the former things have passed away,"* **Verse 4**.

Yes, God has made "all things new," and this act of creation is done. *"And He said to me, 'It is done!' I am the Alpha and the Omega, the Beginning and the End. I will give of the fountain of the water of life freely to him who thirsts. He who overcomes shall inherit all things, and I will be his God and he shall be My son,"* **Verses 6-7, NKJV**.

In **Revelation 1:8, 11 & 17,** Jesus tells John: *" 'I am the Alpha and the Omega, the Beginning and the End,' says the Lord, 'who is and who was and who is to come, the Almighty.' "* Now He reminds John of His previous statement.

This is glorious but there is a reminder of who is not there: *"But the cowardly, unbelieving, abominable, murderers, sexually immoral, sorcerers, idolaters, and all liars shall have their part in the lake which burns with fire and brimstone, which is the second death,"* **Revelation 21:8 NKJV**. This group was judged as liars and cast into the place that God had prepared especially for Satan, the **Liar**, and his angels. Those cast into the lake of fire at the Great White Throne Judgment went there as intruders, for the lake of fire, Hell, was not created for them. **Matthew**

25:41: *"Then He will also say to those on the left hand, 'Depart from Me, you cursed, into the everlasting fire prepared for the devil and his angels."* **NKJV.**

Verses 9 – 21

The New Jerusalem described

Now comes the hard part to describe.

"Then one of the seven angels who had the seven bowls filled with the seven last plagues came to me and talked with me, saying, 'Come, I will show you the bride, the Lamb's wife.' And he carried me away in the Spirit to a great and high mountain, and showed me the great city, the holy Jerusalem, descending out of heaven from God, having the glory of God. Her light was like a most precious stone, like a jasper stone, clear as crystal." **Verse 9 NKJV.**

John is taken to a great mountain on the New Earth. It was huge, it was tall, and it gave him the visual point to see this unbelievable city. This city is where God will dwell with man and where man will worship God and see Him in all His glory. This will be done in a way that is impossible now on this earth because of sin. Everything on the new earth is sin free, pure holy. We will be holy as God is holy. We will have drawn close to God, and now He is drawing close to us. **James 4:7 & 1 Peter 1:16** are seen in a new and pure light: *"Draw near to God and He will draw near to you."* and *"because it is written, 'Be holy, for I am holy."* **NKJV**.

In this New Jerusalem where God dwells, we have been made holy to worship the Holy God Almighty. What John sees is unbelievable. John sees a brilliantly-lit city which had a reddish hue like the jasper stone but clear as a crystal, perhaps to remind us of the precious blood of Jesus.

The walls are massive. Walls are usually made for protection or to keep something out, but there is no need for any of this. The walls are there perhaps to define its limits. There are three gates on each of the four walls, twelve gates in all. Each gate has a name and the name is for the twelve tribes of Israel. The name is engraved above the gate, **Verses 12-13**.

Not only were there twelve gates, but upon the walls there have been placed twelve glorious fountains, and each of these twelve fountains were named for each of the twelve apostles of the Lamb, **Verse 14.**

The angel had a golden measuring reed, **Verse 15**, which he was to use to measure the height, width, and depth of this massive city. The city was a cube, as tall as it was wide, and as deep as well. It was a reminder of the Holy of Holies in the Temple being a cube in its dimensions, **1 Kings 6:20**.

The measurement of the walls of the New Jerusalem was 144 cubits, according to the standard measurement of man. This measurement translates to 12,000 furlongs or 1,400 miles high, wide and deep.

To give one an idea of this great city, consider this: If the New Jerusalem was placed within the borders of the United States, it would stretch from Canada to Mexico and from the Appalachian Mountains to the California coast.

The foundation of the walls of the city had seven layers.

1. The first was jasper—reddish.
2. The second was sapphire—blue.
3. The third was chalcedony—veins of light blue and white.
4. The fourth was emerald—green.
5. The fifth was sardonyx—hues of brown and tan.

6. The sixth was sardius—orangish.
7. The seventh was chrysolite—various hues of green.
8. The eighth was beryl—light blue.
9. The ninth was jacinth—a medium blue.
10. The tenth was chrysoprase—golden yellowish green.
11. The eleventh was jacinth—blue, reddish or violet.
12. The twelfth was amethyst—a light purple.

All the colors of the rainbow can be seen here. The foundation glowed in the brilliance of the light of God.

Adding to the wonder are the twelve gates, which are massive and are made of one pearl. Now that is a big pearl, not produced by an oyster, but prepared by God for this very purpose. As one enters through the gates of pearl, the streets of the city are seen. These streets are pure and transparent gold, as clear as glass. Everything beams and glows with the pure light and glory of God.

Verses 22 – 27

Further glory is seen.

The odd thing about this city is that there was no Temple, no Tabernacle. Why? Because Almighty God and the Lamb are the Temple, the place of worship, and the one to whom all worship is directed. He is visibly present.

The city shines in His light and there is no night there at all. There are kings of this New Earth and people of all nations within the New Earth, and everyone comes to give honor, praise, and glory to the only One worthy of it, as they join in glad worship to our Great God, **Verses 22 – 25**.

The gates remain always open and the city is always bustling with the worshippers of God worshipping God. There is nothing in existence that could bring dishonor to God. The only inhabitants of this New Earth and the New Jerusalem are those whose names have been written in the Lamb's Book of Life. What a glorious day that will be!

Chapter 22

Verses 1 – 5

The River of Life

In **Revelation 2:7** Jesus tells John: *"He who has an ear, let him hear what the Spirit says to the churches. To him who overcomes I will give to eat from tree of life, which is in the midst of the Paradise of God."* **NKJV**. John now sees coming from the very throne of God a crystal-clear river that flows and bubbles freely and constantly from God's Throne. The river runs down the middle of the golden street and on each side of the river of life is the tree of life. This is the tree of life that was taken from Adam for his sin but is here planted by God for us.

The tree of life bears twelve different and delicious fruits. The fruits are different every month, and they are always ripe and ready to eat and good to eat. The leaves of the tree of life are for the healing of the nations. This does not mean that people will get sick or angry with each other. It means that there will never be a disease or a bad feeling ever at any time. The curse of sin is gone, leaving only the blessings of God given to the redeemed by our good, glorious, and faithful God. He is worshipped by the redeemed ones. He alone is worshipped by His redeemed people.

We will have the glorious name of God written upon our heads. Wherever we go and with whomever we might meet, the thing that will be noticed first is the name of God, our Redeemer, written clearly upon our heads.

We will always serve God and He will always care for us forever and ever. John is reminded that there will never be night there in that city, and God alone will be its Light.

Verses 6 – 11

The challenge is given for us today.

Here we have the credibility of what John has witnessed and its validity. **Verse 6:** *"Then he said to me, 'These words are faithful and true.' And the Lord God of the holy prophets sent His angel to show His servants the things which must shortly take place. 'Behold, I am coming quickly! Blessed is he who keeps the words of the prophecy of this book.' "* **NKJV.**

What John has heard is approved by Jesus Himself. Everything that has been revealed to John and every word spoken can be trusted as being true. What has been revealed are things that will happen shortly, and when they begin to take place the events will quickly evolve.

This vision of John was revealed to him around **A. D. 90.** Believers throughout time have kept their eyes focused on the horizon, looking for the coming of Christ Jesus. Why has the Lord not come? Jesus has not come because the time has not arrived. God is not affected by time, but He is all about timing. The time has not fully come. God only moves in the fullness of time.

Galatians 4:4 *"But when the fullness of the time had come, God sent forth His Son, born of a woman, born under the law, to redeem those who were under the law, that we might receive the adoption as sons."* **NKJV.**

2 Peter 3:9 *"The Lord is not slack concerning His promise, as some count slackness, but is longsuffering toward us, not willing that any should perish but that all should come to repentance,"* **NKJV.**

God's patience is a marvelous thing. He does not want any person to be denied all the necessary time he needs to make a personal choice for salvation or to reject His free salvation. Anyone who dies without Christ Jesus does so having every moment necessary to freely chose Jesus or to reject Him. God knows every person who was ever born, and He will reveal Himself to that person. God can reveal himself to anyone seeking Him. There is no one who has ever been born who has had a desire to know God to whom God has not made Himself known. God is ever present. God knows just how long a person needs to make a perfect choice to receive Him or reject Him. When that fullness of time arrives, He will send His Son. This is a true and faithful saying.

Jesus can be counted on because he is faithful and true, but Satan is faithful in another way. He can be counted upon to lie to you and to cause doubt in your mind about God being true. But God is true and all else is a lie. Don't believe the lie; believe the Truth.

John, upon hearing these final few words from the angel, is overcome with awe and falls to his feet to worship the angel. The angel quickly picks him up and chastens him for his action. *"Then he said to me, 'See that you do not do that. For I am your fellow servant, and of your brethren the prophets, and of those who keep the words of this book. Worship God.' "* **Verse 9, NKJV.**

The angel tells John to get this book out to believers to let them know what has been revealed to him. Time is of the essence. Warn the unjust, encourage the just, reprove the filthy and commend the righteous. Inspire the holy ones to strive to be holier still. Don't be satisfied with where you are in your life. Press on toward the high calling of God and carry the Good News.

Paul wrote in **Acts 20:24:** *"But none of these things move me; nor do I count my life dear to myself, so that I may finish my race with joy, and the ministry which I received from the Lord Jesus, to testify to the gospel of the grace of God."* **NKJV.**

Jesus said, *"Go therefore and make disciples of all the nations, baptizing them in the name of the Father and of the Son and of the Holy Spirit, teaching them to observe all things that I have commanded you; and low I am with you always, even to the end of the age."* **Matthew 28:19-20 NKJV.**

The end of the age will soon come. We all must be ready. Are you ready?

"Blessed are those who do His commandments, that they may have the right to the tree of life, and may enter through the gates into the city." **Verse 14, NKJV.**

Remember, dear reader, God is for you but all else is against you. Satan is alive and well on this green earth right now. He dogs you down. He seeks you out and will do all within his power to keep you from Christ Jesus. Listen to the still small voice within you and come to Him, and He will forgive your sin and give you eternal life.

Jesus, is speaking to you right now: *" 'I, Jesus, have sent My angel to testify to you these things in the churches. I am the Root and the Offspring of David, the Bright and Morning Star.' And the Spirit and the bride say, 'Come!' And let him who hears say, 'Come!' And let him who thirsts come. Whoever desires, let him take the water of life freely."* **Verse 16, NKJV.**

Verses 18 – 19

There is a warning to anyone who teaches this book of **Revelation** and that is if anyone adds anything to what God has revealed through John, or if he takes away anything from what has been revealed, then God will take away that person's part in the Book of Life. That person will not be allowed into His New Heaven, New Earth and New Jerusalem.

Verses 20 & 21

Jesus says, "Surely I am coming and I will come quickly." To which John affirms, *"Amen. Even so, come, Lord Jesus!"* **Verse 20, NKJV.**

The last words of John are: "The grace of our Lord Jesus Christ be with you all. Amen." **Verse 21, NKJV.**

Thanks be to God for His great grace and marvelous mercy which He offers to those who believe Him; to those who believe Him to be God's Only Begotten Son and soon coming King. He will soon return for those who believe in Him. May you learn as you read.

Conclusion

The Bible begins with: *"In the beginning God created the heavens and the earth. The earth was without form and void; and darkness was on the face of the deep. And the Spirit of God was hovering over the face of the waters."* **Genesis 1:1-2 NKJV**. The Bible concludes with: *"The grace of our Lord Jesus Christ be with you all. Amen."* **Revelation 22:21 NKJV.**

God created a perfect world in the beginning but after that, Satan entered God's wondrous creation and polluted it with the lie of sin. God then promised a Redeemer, and that is what we find fulfilled in the book of Revelation. God now makes all things new and judges Satan, the Liar. Satan is a liar and all those who follow him are the sons of the Liar. Jesus said in **John 8:44:** *"You are of your father the devil, and the desires of your father you want to do. He was a murderer from the beginning, and does not stand in the truth, because there is no truth in him. When he speaks a lie, he speaks from his own resources, for he is a liar and the father of it."* **NKJV**.

God does not want any person to die in his or her sin. The reason He came was to offer life for death. Still, most of humanity will reject His free gift. All who are not believers in Christ Jesus will be cast, as intruders, into a special place that God has prepared for Satan and his angels. **Matthew 25:41:** *"Then He will also say to those on the left hand, 'Depart from Me, you cursed, into the everlasting fire prepared for the devil and his angels."* **NKJV**. **Revelation 20:14:** *"Then Death and Hades were cast into the lake of fire. This is the second death. And anyone not found written in the Book of Life was cast into the lake of fire."* **NKJV**. **Revelation 21:8:** *"But the cowardly, unbelieving, abominable, murderers, sexually immoral,* *sorcerers, idolaters, and <u>all liars</u> shall have their part in the lake which burns with fire and brimstone, which is the second death."* **NKJV**.

We have read in **Revelation 21:5:** *"Then He who sat on the throne said, 'Behold, I make all things new.' And He said to me, 'Write, for these words are true and faithful.' And He said to me, 'It is done! I am the Alpha and the Omega, the Beginning and the End. I will give of the fountain of the water of life freely to him who thirsts. He who overcomes shall inherit all things, and I will be his God and he shall be My son.' "* **NKJV**.

From the Beginning to the End, from the Alpha to the Omega, we see Jesus and watch as He works His great plan for our good and His glory. Truly God's great grace and mercy has been unveiled and revealed to all who would have an ear to hear and an eye to read what has been written.

There is also a warning, which is in **22:19:** *"and if anyone takes away from the words of the book of this prophecy, God shall take away his part from the Book of Life, from the holy city, and from the things which are written in this book."* **NKJV**.

"The task of the scholar is to guarantee the purity of the text, to get as close as possible to the Word as originally given. He may compare Scripture with Scripture until He discovers the true meaning of the text. But right there his authority ends. He must never sit in judgment upon what is written. He must not bring the meaning of the Word before the bar of his reason.' – **found written inside the cover of my dad's first preaching Bible.**

This is what I have attempted to do. I want to display Jesus as The Truth and Satan as The Liar. What is more opposite than The Truth and The Lie? Jesus is The Truth and Satan is The Liar. The lie denies the Truth, questions the Truth, and the Truth refutes and exposes the Lie. The lie bends the Truth to appear to be less than the Truth. The lie claims to be the ruth, and it is not. The lie hides the Truth, clouds the Truth, aTnd adds to the Truth to create doubt.

The Truth denies the lie, brings light to the lie, and needs nothing else or no one else to substantiate it as Truth. The Truth remains the Truth, the whole Truth, and nothing but the Truth. Any shade of turning from the Truth is a lie. Yes, Satan is the father of the lie.

Jesus is the Truth and came into this world to bring the Truth, and enlighten us to the Truth. He came to bring light into the darkness, although most would reject Him. They reject Him because their deeds are evil. If they do come to the Light, they expose their evil deeds. **John 3:16 – 21:** *"For God so loved the world that He gave His only begotten Son, that whoever believes in Him should not perish but have everlasting life. For God did not send His Son into the world to condemn the world, but that the world through Him might be saved. He who believes in Him is not condemned; but he who does not believe is condemned already, because he has not believed in the name of the only begotten Son of God. And this is the condemnation, that the light has come into the world, and men loved darkness rather than light, because their deeds were evil. For everyone practicing evil hates the light and does not come to the light, lest his deeds should be exposed. But he who does the truth comes to the light, that his deeds may be clearly seen, that they have been done in God."* **NKJV**.

What you have read is JUST THE BASICS. Study, read, and share. Read from the Scripture every day, and then share what you have read from Scripture with someone every day. This too is just the BASIC duty of every believer as well. It is all about Him and them.

Danny G. Thomas

Alpha and Omega

" 'I am the Alpha and Omega, the Beginning and the End,' says the Lord, 'who is and who was and who is to come, the Almighty.' " **Revelation 1:8 NKJV**. Jesus says that He is the Alpha and Omega, (Alpha being the first letter of the Greek Alphabet and Omega being the last one.), and that He is the beginning and the end. He is the first and the last, the Only Begotten Son of God.

John begins his gospels with: *"In the beginning was the Word, and the Word was with God, and the Word was God. He was in the beginning with God. All things were made through Him, and without Him nothing was made that was made. In Him was life, and the life was the light of men. And the light shines in the darkness, and the darkness did not comprehend it."* **John 1:1-5 NKJV**.

John also begins his epistle of **1 John** in a similar fashion: *"That which was from the beginning, which we have heard, which we have seen with our eyes, which we have looked upon, and our hands have handled, concerning the Word of life—the life was manifested, and we have seen, and bear witness, and declare to you that eternal life which was with the Father and was manifested to us—"* **1 John 1:1-2 NKJV**.

Scripture begins with the beginning, the Alpha: *"In the beginning God created the heavens and the earth. The earth was without form, and void; and darkness was on the face of the deep. And the Spirit of God was hovering over the face of the waters. Then God said, 'Let there be light', and there was light. . . . Then God said, 'Let us make man in Our image, according to Our likeness; let them have dominion over the fish of the sea, over the birds of the air, and over the cattle, over all the earth and over every creeping thing that creeps on the earth. So, God created man in His own image; in the image of God He created him; male and female He created them."* **Genesis 1:1-3 & 26-27 NKJV**.

We read of God's complete understanding of various men who God knew completely before they were created:

Jeremiah records: *"Before I formed you in the womb I knew you; before you were born I sanctified you; I ordained you a prophet to the nations."* **Jeremiah 1:5 NKJV**.

David makes note: *"Your eyes saw my substance being yet unformed. And in Your book, they all were written, the days fashioned for me, when as yet there were none of them."* **Psalm 139:16 NKJV**.

Frequently we read statements such as: *"before the foundations of the world." "Blessed be the God and Father of our Lord Jesus Christ, who has blessed us with every spiritual blessing in the heavenly places in Christ, just as He chose us in Him before the foundations of the world, that we should be holy and without blame before Him in love, having predestined us to adoption as sons by Jesus Christ to Himself, according to the good pleasure of His will."* **Ephesians 1:3-5 NKJV**.

God is the Creator of all. He created mankind, the earth, the universe and all that is in it. Everything has a beginning; everything is finite. Only God is without beginning or end for He is eternal, infinite. Mankind cannot understand the thought of not having a beginning point or a birth, but we like to think that we will not end. The truth is, everyone will spend eternity somewhere, either in heaven, a place God has created for those who "believe in Him" or in hell which was created for Satan and his angels.

This is a mystery which cannot be understood by man but the creation need not understand the Creator. He must only know the Creator, believe the Creator, and place his hope in the Creator who knows all things.

It is impossible to live eternally in heaven with God unless one has been <u>born again,</u> just as it is impossible to live on this physical earth without being born physically. There is only one way for each. Jesus expressed to Nicodemus: *"Jesus answered and said to him, 'Most assuredly, I say to you, unless one is born again, he cannot see the kingdom of God.' Nicodemus said to Him, 'How can a man be born when he is old? Can he enter a second time into his mother's womb and be born?' Jesus answered, 'Most assuredly, I say to you, unless one is born <u>of water</u>* (physical birth) *and the Spirit, he cannot enter the kingdom of God. That which is born of the flesh is flesh, and that which is born of the Spirit is spirit."* **John 3:3-7 NKJV**.

New birth comes by faith or believing Jesus to be who He said He is. God then delivers His forgiveness and applies to the believer faith, mercy, and grace, and he will not die eternally. **John 3:16b:** *"that whoever believes in Him should not perish but have everlasting life."* **NKJV**.

So, being born on this sinful earth carries with it a physical death penalty:

- **Hebrews 9:27:** *"And as it is appointed for men to die once, but after this the judgment,"* **NKJV**. Paul writes of all humanity being born into sin and that the penalty for sin is death.

Paul writes:

- **Romans 3:23:** *"for all have sinned and fall short of the glory of God."* **NKJV**.

- **Romans 6:23:** *"For the wages of sin is death, but the gift of God is eternal life in Christ Jesus our Lord."* **NKJV**.

That is the shocking news, but there is Good News! There is an option, a choice, that God has provided for His creation, which is that it is not necessary to die spiritually or to suffer death a second time. The Father sent His Only Begotten Son, Jesus, to pay the penalty for sin, and He conquered sin death, and the grave. **1 Corinthians 15:51-58:** *"Behold, I tell you a mystery: We shall not all sleep, but we shall all be changed—in a moment, in the twinkling of an eye, at the last trumpet. For the trumpet will sound, and the dead will be raised incorruptible, and we shall be changed. For this corruptible must put on incorruption, and this mortal must put on immortality. So, when this corruptible has put on incorruption, and this mortal has put on immortality, then shall be brought to pass the saying that is written: 'Death is swallowed up in victory.' "O Death, where is your sting? O Hades, where is your victory?' The sting of death is sin, and the strength of sin is the law. But thanks be to God, who gives us the victory through our Lord Jesus Christ. Therefore, my beloved brethren, be steadfast, immovable, always abounding in the work of the Lord, knowing that your labor is not in vain in the Lord."* **NKJV**.

John addresses the second death:

- **Revelation 20:14-15 NKJV**: *"Then Death and Hades were cast into the lake of fire. This is the second death. And anyone not found written in the Book of Life was cast into the lake of fire."*

- **Revelation 19:5 & 6** *"But the rest of the dead did not live again until the thousand years were finished. This is the first resurrection. Blessed and holy is he who has part in the first resurrection. Over such the second death has no power, but they shall be priests of God and of Christ, and shall reign with Him a thousand years."* **NKJV**.

Jesus addresses the second death and the purpose of hell:

- **Matthew 25:31-46:** *"When the Son of Man comes in His glory, and all the holy angels with Him, then He will sit on the throne of His glory. All the nations will be gathered before Him, and He will separate them one from another ... then He will also say to those on the left hand, 'Depart from Me, you cursed, into the everlasting fire prepared for the devil and his angels ... And these will go away into everlasting punishment, but the righteous into eternal life."* **NKJV**.

Did you notice that Hell was not created for man but for, *"the devil and his angels"?* If God's created mankind goes there, he will go as an intruder, in that hell was not created for mankind. Mankind has a choice regarding his eternity, and that choice is eternal life or eternal death.

Jesus also told His disciples just before He was to be crucified: *"Let not your heart be troubled, you believe in God, believe also in Me. In My Father's house are many mansions, if it were not so, I would have told you, I go to prepare a place for you, and if I go and prepare a place for you, I will come again and receive you to Myself; that where I am there you may be also."* **John 14:1-3 NKJV**.

Jesus told Nicodemus in **John 3:16b:** **"***whoever believes in Him should not perish but have everlasting life,"* or will not die eternally. Now understand that everyone who is born will die once, physically (**Hebrews 9:27:** *"And it is appointed for men to die once, but after this the judgment,"* **NKJV**), but it is not necessary to die spiritually or the second time.

John writes of the second death:

- **Revelation 20:5-6:** *"But the rest of the dead did not live again until the thousand years were finished. This is the first resurrection. Blessed and holy is he who has* *part in the first resurrection. Over such the second death has no power, but they shall be priests of God and of Christ, and shall reign with Him a thousand years."* **NKJV**.

- **Revelation 20:14-15 NKJV**: *"Then Death and Hades were cast into the lake of fire. This is the second death. And anyone not found written in the Book of Life was cast into the lake of fire."*

What God has done is to make the believer a New Creation.

- **2 Corinthians 5:17** *"Therefore, if anyone is in Christ, he is a new creation, old things have passed away; behold, all things have become new."* **NKJV**.

- **2 Corinthians 5:21** *"For He made Him who knew no sin to be sin for us, that we might become the righteousness of God in Him."* **NKJV**.

I like to describe this "new creation" in this manner: At creation, God took <u>nothing and made something</u>; when we become a "new creation" God takes <u>something</u>, our sin, and makes <u>nothing</u>, a sinless creation. Old things have passed away and all things have become new. So, as the believer stands before God, He sees the righteousness of His Only Begotten Son, Jesus. We look just like Him.

This new life is eternal life. The believer then will never die a second death.

I have prepared a chart of eternity past and future, and to trace time, its beginning, its end, and how creation fits into it.

God, the creator of all, <u>is</u> eternal. As I have said earlier, God has no beginning nor has He an end. God just **_is_.** God says of Himself, "I Am God." *"<u>I am</u> the Lord, and there is no other; There is no God besides Me."* **Isaiah 45:5 NKJV**.

When Moses asked God what was His name, God's answer to him was: *"Then Moses said to God, 'Indeed, when I come to the children of Israel and say to them, 'The God of your fathers has sent me to you,' and they say to me, 'What is His name?' what shall I say to them?' And God said to Moses, 'I AM WHO I AM. And He said, 'Thus you shall say to the children of Israel, 'I AM has sent me to you.'"* **Exodus 3:13-14 NKJV**.

Here is the point: There can only be one God, one Prime Mover, one Supreme One. Supreme means top or superior and above all others. Just as there are many courts, but only one Supreme Court and it is above all the rest, there is one Supreme Being and that is God.

Though many people question God, He does not have to prove Himself because "He Is Truth." Science is a search for truth, God is Truth. Truth is the measure of all else. Truth is fact. Truth can be questioned, but the question has no validity for it is not Truth.

My Mother had Alzheimer's disease and was plagued with many delusions which she thought were true. She lived in great fear of these delusions which were not true. They were lies. Because this disease caused her to be irrational, there was no way to bring her to the truth. She did not have the ability to reason. So, she lived her life in the fear of a lie. God is Truth, and any irrational thought is nothing but a lie. In order for a person to come to the Truth, he must acknowledge the Truth as Truth.

God is also Eternal, Sovereign and Supreme. God is without beginning and without end. Time began with sin against God and time will end with the judgment by God. God was before time, and He will continue through time and emerge beyond its conclusion.

Remember, God created the angels, and this includes Satan for he is an angel. God created the earth, the universe, and everything in it, however small or large. God has created things that can be seen by the eye and those things that are unseen or too small for the eye to see. God knows all things as well—those things that are known and understood by the human mind and those things that are unknown to the human mind. There is nothing that God does not know, and He has always known them. We cannot know all things but God does. We cannot have the mind of God, but we can have the mind of Christ within us. God stands alone and above all.

Time Line, Part One.

The Plan of God, How It All Fits Together.

Pre-existent God, Angels, Creation, Sin, Pre-flood Mankind
and Flood

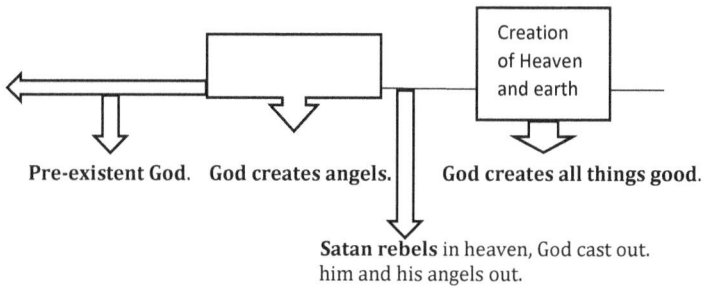

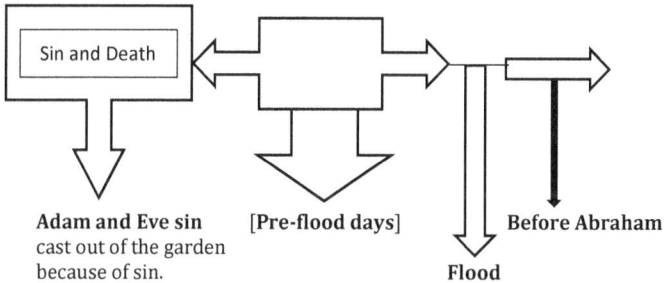

Creation
of Heaven
and earth

Pre-existent God. **God creates angels.**   **God creates all things good.**

Satan rebels in heaven, God cast out.
him and his angels out.

Sin and Death

Adam and Eve sin   **[Pre-flood days]**   **Before Abraham**
cast out of the garden
because of sin.   **Flood**

"Promise of the Messiah"
Genesis 3:15

Time Line, Part Two.

Abraham, Israel, The First Coming of Christ, Crucifixion, Resurrection, Ascension, Church Age and Rapture.

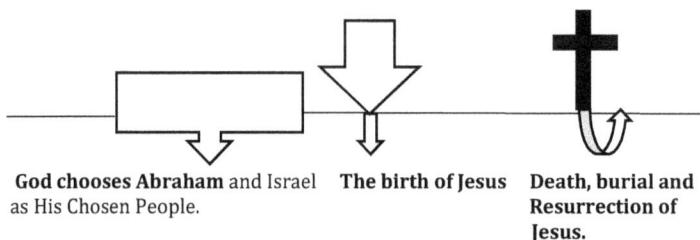

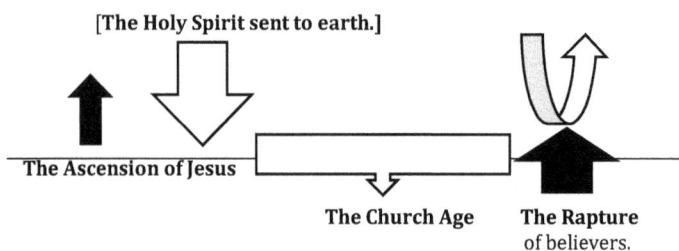

God chooses Abraham and Israel as His Chosen People.   **The birth of Jesus**   **Death, burial and Resurrection of Jesus.**

[The Holy Spirit sent to earth.]

The Ascension of Jesus

The Church Age   **The Rapture** of believers.
They meet the Lord in the air and **The Holy Spirit is taken out of the earth**. At that very moment, there are no followers of Christ on earth for they have been taken up to meet Christ Jesus in the air.

Time Line, Part Three.

The Tribulation, Second Coming, Satan imprisoned, Millennial Reign of Christ, Satan's release and final rebellion.

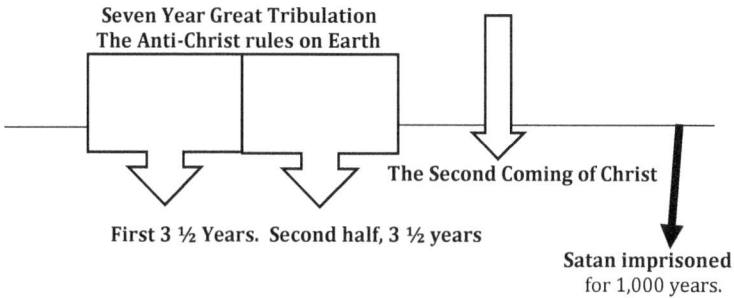

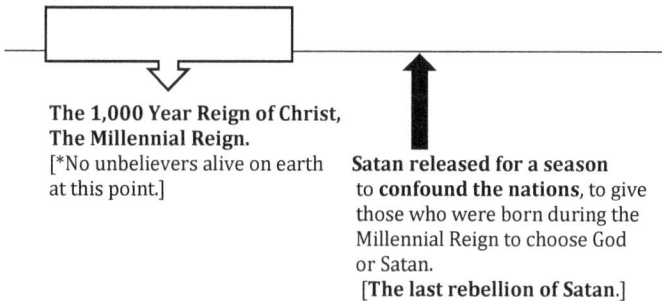

Seven Year Great Tribulation
The Anti-Christ rules on Earth

The Second Coming of Christ

First 3 ½ Years. Second half, 3 ½ years

Satan imprisoned
for 1,000 years.

The 1,000 Year Reign of Christ,
The Millennial Reign.
[*No unbelievers alive on earth
at this point.]

Satan released for a season
to **confound the nations**, to give
those who were born during the
Millennial Reign to choose God
or Satan.
[**The last rebellion of Satan.**]

Time Line, Part Four.

Satan and His Angels Cast into Hell, Great White Throne Judgment, The New Heaven, New Earth, and New Jerusalem and eternity.

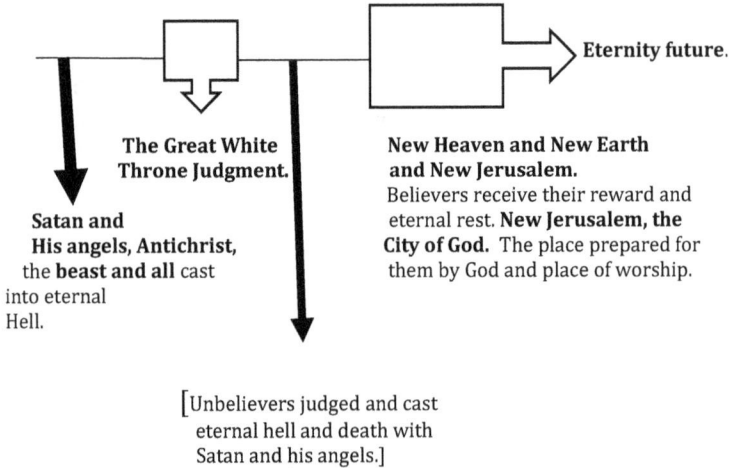

Eternity future.

The Great White Throne Judgment.

Satan and His angels, Antichrist, the **beast and all** cast into eternal Hell.

New Heaven and New Earth and New Jerusalem. Believers receive their reward and eternal rest. **New Jerusalem, the City of God.** The place prepared for them by God and place of worship.

[Unbelievers judged and cast eternal hell and death with Satan and his angels.]